Minding Your Own Business

The Solo and Small Firm Lawyer's Guide to a Profitable Practice

ANN M. GUINN

INVOICE

INVOICE # [100]
DATE: DECEMBER 9, 2009

OVERDUE

DUE DATE

AMERICAN BAR ASSOCIATION
General Practice,
Solo & Small Firm
Division

Cover design by ABA Publishing

Page Layout by Quadrum Solutions (www.quadrumltd.com)

Printed in the United States of America.

14 13 12 11 10   5 4 3 2 1

Library of Congress Cataloging-in-Publication Data

Guinn, Ann M., 1948-

  Essential management guide for the solo and small firm practitioner: minding your business / Ann M. Guinn.
        p. cm.
  Includes bibliographical references and index.
  ISBN 978-1-60442-939-8 (alk. paper)
  1. Solo law practice—United States. 2. Law offices—United States. 3. Practice of law—United States. I. Title.
  KF318.G85 2010
  340.068—dc22

2010011603

Dedication

I can do all things through He who strengthens me. (Phil. 4:13)

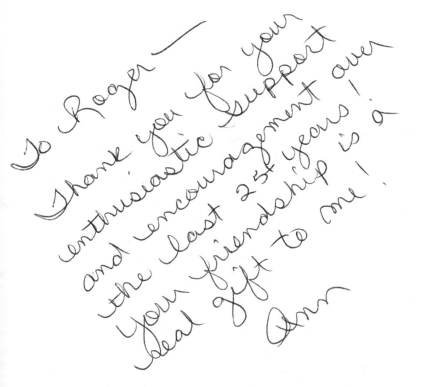

To Roger—
Thank you for your
enthusiastic support
and encouragement over
the last 25 years!
Your friendship is a
deal gift to me!
Ann

Table of Contents

Acknowledgements

A book like this doesn't just happen. In the popular vernacular, it takes a village. I owe a debt of gratitude beyond measure to a number of people, and I want to thank them publicly here.

First, I cannot begin to express my thanks to my Mom and my Dad for their unfailing support and encouragement in my life, in general, and in the writing of this book, in particular. Thank you for believing that I'm far more accomplished than I am.

To my brothers David and Steve—your love and friendship is a blessed gift to me. I love you right back.

To Lou for pushing me to write this book, and for helping me over the rough spots. I couldn't have done this without you.

To Grandma and Grandpa Jordan—you were wrong. I wasn't the smartest grandchild ever born, but I know you'd still be proud.

To DJR, who taught me to be a darned good legal secretary, and let me test my limits on a daily basis. I owe my entire legal career to you.

To my dear friend Ellen, who during 38 years has taught me how to cite check, make Norwegian meatballs, and accept that "Ufda" is a complete sentence.

To my dear friend and former business partner Deanna, who helped me follow my dream of starting my own business. It would never have worked without you. Thank you!

To my precious friends Charlene, Donna, Chris, Patty and Kay—you are the cheerleaders in my life. I have done nothing to deserve your unfailing friendship, but I am eternally grateful that you have offered it to me without reservation.

To Pinky, Maggie, Ferdie, Sarah and Benny—you've been my greatest joys in life. Your unconditional love and your warm, furry bodies have never failed to restore my spirits.

A sky-high thank-you to Kathleen Hopkins, who e-mailed a total stranger one day and said, "How would you like to write a book for the ABA?" You have truly been my angel through this entire process.

To my ever-patient editor Rick Paszkeit. When you said, "I've read your first three chapters, and I love what I see" you gave me the courage to write a book that I never thought I could do. And, the praise kept coming. Thank you!

Lastly, to my wonderful, amazing, hard-working clients – this book would never have happened without you. You've taught me more than you will ever know with your personal stories, your perseverance, and your willingness to work on the business of law. Beyond our professional relationship, I treasure your friendship. Thank you, one and all.

There are so many others who deserve my thanks, and I'm sure I've inadvertently overlooked someone who has been critical to my development. Please accept my sincere apologies for the oversight. I'll make it up to you in the next book!

INTRODUCTION

For three or four years, I had "Write a book" on my annual list of goals. And, there it safely sat, year after year, until an unbelievable opportunity came along. The ABA asked me to write a book. I don't know why–no one at the ABA had ever heard of me. I was stunned! Nevertheless, I took this as a sign that I was to take "Write a book" off my goals list and put it on my "to-do" list. That was the easy part. Getting the lessons I've learned from 30+ years in the legal field down on paper was the killer. Sharing the stories of small firm practitioners just like you became my total focus. I wanted so badly to get it right, tell it like it is, and offer hope because I knew that one day, you would pick up this book and look to it for answers. It isn't perfect, and I may not have covered everything you need to hear; but, please know that I'm on your side, and I've done the very best I could for you. I hope it helps!

Ann Guinn
February 2010

1

NOT JUST AN ATTORNEY:
THE THREE ROLES OF A SMALL FIRM PRACTITIONER

"It was a dark and stormy night. Suddenly, a shot rang out! A door slammed. The maid screamed.

"Suddenly, a pirate ship appeared on the horizon!

"While millions of people were starving, the king lived in luxury. Meanwhile, on a small farm in Kansas, a boy was growing up" – to be a solo practitioner.

Author – Snoopy (with help from Ann Guinn)

Ah, that nurturing mothers and wisdom-sharing fathers across the country were growing their children to be not just attorneys, but solo or small firm practitioners to boot. The sad truth of the matter is that nobody helps grow solo and small firm practitioners—not parents, not public school, not law school; yet, well over half the attorneys in the U.S. practice in a solo or small firm, and most of these attorneys are managing the business, as well.

When asked, few attorneys will say that they entered law school with the idea of one day running their own small practice; however, life happens, and now they find themselves trying to practice law and manage a business at the same time. Rather, they may have envisioned themselves defending the freedoms guaranteed in the U.S. Constitution, but not struggling to calculate overtime pay for staff. They may be committed to insuring that our legal system works, but not so interested in developing marketing strategies to attract new business. They may spend hours on pro bono work to help provide access to justice for all—and even more hours trying to analyze the firm's financial statements to spot ways to reduce overhead expenses. They may be comfortable arguing a case in court, but way out of their element coaching an employee.

The fact is that solo and small firm attorneys are frequently handling business-related tasks for which they have had little or no training. Funny, isn't it, that arguing a case with no legal training is a violation of the law, but running a law firm with no business training isn't. In either situation, you can easily harm your clients.

As a practice management consultant to solo and small firms, I believe that the practice of law is a business <u>and</u> a profession—and small firm practitioners are, first, business managers, and second, attorneys. The business provides the framework and support necessary to enable the attorney to practice law. Through ***good financial management***, the business makes sure the attorney gets paid. Through the implementation of various ***marketing strategies***, the business brings in new clients for the attorney to serve. Through a steadfast ***focus on the needs of the client***, the business insures that clients are well served and satisfied. By ***providing the practitioner with trained staff***, and technological aids in the form of practice-specific software, PDAs, on-line research, and much more, the business helps the attorney be as productive and efficient as possible.

Let's look at how the small firm practitioner makes this happen.

The three roles of a small firm practitioner.

To be successful, you must understand and fulfill various roles in your business. Michael Gerber did a great job of identifying the three roles of a small business owner in his best-selling book, *The E-Myth Revisited: Why Most Small Businesses Don't Work and What To Do About It.*

The problem is that everybody who goes into business is actually three-people-in-one. The Entrepreneur. The Manager. The Technician. And the problem is compounded by the fact that while each of these personalities wants to be the boss, none of them wants to have a boss. So, they start a business together in order to get rid of the boss. And the conflict begins.

Let's consider what these three roles look like in a law firm:

1. *The entrepreneur*—The person with the dream, the vision of what the practice can become. You set the course for the firm to follow. If you don't have a definite plan, the firm will be forced to find its own way—and, as I am fond of saying, "If you don't know where you're going, you'll probably end up somewhere else." Circumstances, trends, clients, economics, etc., will shape a business without a vision and a plan. No vision, no goal, no plan—no recipe for success.

I frequently ask attorneys to describe where they see their firms in two years, five years, and 10 years from now. In 18 years of asking, I can count on one hand the number of attorneys who had given much thought at all to the future of the firm, other than that it will still be in existence. I remember vividly the day I asked a 60-something-year-old attorney where she planned to be in five years. She looked completely stunned and then blurted out, "I just assumed I would be dead." I guess that's a plan, too, but it wouldn't be my first choice!

Entrepreneurs aren't locked into tradition—they dream of what might be. They live in the future, think outside the box, take calculated risks, are willing to make mistakes, and see opportunity all around them.

Take a moment to test your visionary skills:

- If your firm could be anything you want it to be, what would that look like?
- What's the craziest idea you've ever had for your practice?
- Did you give it a try?
- How did it work out?
- If you didn't try it, what held you back?
- What do you want to be known for?
- What do you need to do to make that happen?
- Describe the best business model you can come up with for a law firm.
- Is that your current business model?
- How can you adopt that model in your own practice?

When considering what might be possible, be aware of what other law firms are doing, but spend more time looking at what other industries are doing. When you copy another law firm's business model, you are not being innovative, and you won't have the competitive edge. Unless you can improve upon their ideas in some meaningful way, you'll always be Avis to their Hertz.

Okay, "How can I get these brilliant new ideas?" you ask. Well, to get new ideas, you have to take in new information from new sources and new experiences.

- Spend time thinking about your business and its future. Where are you now, where do you want to go, and how will you get there? Go on an annual retreat. Spend a couple of days by yourself away from distractions (that means Las Vegas is out, a quiet resort in off season is in). All you need is a yellow legal pad and a pen.
- Do something you wouldn't ordinarily do, try something you wouldn't ordinarily try. Rent a movie you've never heard of, try ordering a new dish at your favorite restaurant, read a book on a topic that is of no interest to you (I borrowed a book

from the library on the history of undergarments—I'd like to tell you that it was uplifting, but it was just plain boring!). Take a new route to work or to another regular destination, read a business magazine, or buy fresh flowers for your desk. You get the picture—shake things up a little. Each new experience will give you new information.

- Watch trends and demographics in your geographic area for new opportunities.

- Check out other service industries. What value-added services does your hairstylist offer? How does your mechanic charge for services? How does your CPA maintain communication with you throughout the year? How do you feel when you're speaking with your doctor? How does your financial advisor market her services? Other service professionals can be a great source of new ideas.

- Refuse to let the "what ifs" or "buts" argue you out of new ideas.

- If you have negative people in your life, don't share your new ideas with them until you've put them into action. Well-meaning, but fearful, friends and family members can quash even the most exciting ideas, and you don't need that.

Envision your dream firm and then stand back and let the Manager in you make it happen.

2. ***The manager***—The person responsible for the day-to-day operations of the firm. The manager keeps the business solvent, staffed, on track, productive, and efficient. Small firms don't have the layered infrastructure found in larger firms; they don't typically have a CFO, marketing director, human resources manager or firm administrator to assume the myriad responsibilities of the manager. In a small firm, the manager typically handles tasks ranging from marketing to coaching employees to analyzing financial statements to collections calls on past-due accounts, and everything in between. As if this weren't enough, the manager must also implement the plan that will help the firm fulfill the vision of the entrepreneur. Sounds like a full-time job, doesn't it? However, in a small firm, the manager is usually a practicing attorney, as well.

It is the role of manager for which most attorneys are ill prepared. Law schools tend not to offer courses on law practice management, and not many post-law school continuing education programs deal with the business side of the practice of law either. That leaves solo and small firm practitioners on their own to figure out how to run a business. Thankfully, there are a great many excellent books dealing with various aspects of business management available through the American Bar Association and your local bookstore. [NOTE: A suggested reading list is included in this book.] In addition, the American Bar Association and a number of state bar associations now sponsor solo/small firm conferences each year. Lucky attorneys find mentors to teach them what they need to know, both about the practice of law and about running a law firm.

3. *The technician*—The person who actually performs the work (the attorney, in a law firm). This is what you trained to do, where your passion lies, where you are most comfortable. For the most part, attorneys just want to practice law. That's what they studied for and that's where their skills lie. I think most attorneys would be happiest if they could just concentrate on the legal work all day long and never give a second thought to a timesheet, a past-due account, or a networking opportunity.

Which of these roles is your favorite? How do you feel about the other two? How much time do you spend in a month in each role? What can you do to get better at handling each of these roles?

I have often noticed a distinct disconnect between the technician and the manager. When I ask a solo practitioner about a current case, the technician becomes quite animated describing the circumstances of the matter and the strategies that will help the client. Let me ask about last year's profit and loss statement, and the technician's brow furrows, a frown appears, and the attorney's whole physical demeanor can change. It's obvious to me which role is most comfortable for the attorney—and, it's usually not that of the manager.

Technicians/attorneys tend to be reactive managers—they often address management issues only when they can no longer be ignored. Unfortunately, reactive management is all about putting out fires, and not about planning for success. Proactive managers develop strategies, have a game plan, anticipate problems and head them off, bring out the best in their employees, and guide the firm. Reactive managers follow behind as external forces, rather than internal strategies, shape the firm.

Proactive managers take charge of the future. Reactive managers are victims of the future.

Would you describe yourself as a proactive or reactive manager? How's that working for you? What could you do better?

Recognizing the three roles that you fill in your small practice is the first step. Learning and accepting the responsibilities of each is the next. Even if you choose to delegate certain of your duties to others, you are ultimately responsible for the well-being and success of your firm. Give every role the time and attention it requires.

Envision your firm's future, plan for its success, and build a business that allows you to practice law in an environment that is supportive and satisfying for you. It's certainly within your reach if you'll attend to the three roles of a solo or small firm practitioner.

> *Tip: If you think just being a good attorney assures success—think again!*

2
YOUR BUSINESS:
WHAT YOU DON'T KNOW COULD HURT YOU

Growing up, I bet your mother told you more than once, "What you don't know can hurt you." She must have had a premonition that one day you would have your own law firm, because truer words were never spoken about the business side of a law practice. What you don't know *can* hurt you.

If you are a brand-new attorney, you don't yet know what you don't know. Don't be embarrassed about this—there are plenty of attorneys with many years of practice under their respective belts who are only now figuring out what they need to know about business—but, don't. I can relate to this. I have a sideline business in antiques, and I have heard many an antiques dealer say, "The longer I'm in this business, the more I realize all that I don't know." The same is true for many small firm attorneys and their businesses.

So, what must a small firm practitioner know about running a successful law practice? Arguably, the most important point is that a law practice is a business. Your legal services? That's your product—what your business sells. Macy's is a business that sells clothing— that's their product. You own a business that sells legal services—that's your product.

The more you understand about your business, the more successful it can become—so, it stands to reason that the less you know about your business, the less successful it will be.

Your business provides the framework and support that allows you to provide your legal services. Law school taught you how to be an attorney (although some might disagree with that statement), but nothing about running a business. It's not until they get out in the real world and open up their small practices that many attorneys begin to learn the business skills necessary to be successful.

Learn all you can about business in general, and about your business in particular. Develop a plan, carefully select your business strategies, and get on intimate terms with your firm's financial statements. Understand your position in the marketplace, hone your marketing skills, become a proactive manager. Never stop learning about business—or about your business.

How well do you really know your business?

"All right, already. I know my business backwards and forwards. So, why isn't it working so well for me now?"

You think you know everything there is to know about your business? Take a minute to answer the following questions, and then let's talk. [NOTE: This is not an open-book quiz!]:

- What were your firm's revenues last week? Expenses?

- What percentage of your revenues goes to expenses annually?

- How many days does it take you to get paid?

- How many months' worth of revenues do you have tied up in accounts receivable?

- How much money is currently tied up in your WIP (work in process)?

- What is your realization rate and that of each of the firm's other timekeepers?

- Does your firm have a written budget, business plan, and marketing plan? When is the last time you reviewed each? Updated each?

- How many hours must you bill in a day to break even?

- How many hours did you bill last year? The other timekeepers?

- What do you expect to bill this year? The other timekeepers?

- Which of your practice areas is most profitable? Least? Are you guessing or do you have actual cost/revenues proof?

- What is the true cost of each of your employees?

- What share of the firm's overhead should be allocated to each timekeeper?

- How often do you review your profit and loss statement? Your balance sheet? Your aged receivables report? What do you do with the information you glean from reviewing financial statements?

- Have you formulated a strategic plan to help you increase revenues over the next five years?

- What trends have you noticed in your overhead expenses over the last five years?

- How do you set your fees? Was your first consideration what your competition is charging?

- How old is the oldest file you have in storage?

- What is your associate attorney and/or legal assistant's long-term career plan and how does your firm fit in?

- What is your best source of new clients? What data have you collected to substantiate this belief? How do you incorporate this valuable information into your marketing strategies?

- Which is your most cost-effective marketing strategy?

- How much does it cost to generate a new client from each of your marketing strategies?

- What do your clients really think of you? Have you asked them? When did you last ask?

- Before you renew your office lease, what are the building owner's long-term plans for the building/your space?

This list could go on and on, but you get the picture. There is so much more to knowing your business than simply looking at the bottom line. You still may not know what all you don't know, but you now have a starting point. Ask your mentors, take classes, attend CLEs on law practice management issues—because you need to know these things. Study other service industries. Read business-related books. Learn, learn, and learn some more. The more you know about the business of the practice of law, the more efficient, productive, profitable, and satisfying your practice will become. Fill in the gaps in your business knowledge and you'll have a good shot at growing the practice of your dreams.

> *Tip: Make minding your own business your top priority!*

WHAT'S WORKING—WHAT'S NOT

To find out how your firm is doing and where you might need to do some work, please take a moment to answer the following questions:

CHECK ONE

Yes	No	
___	___	Do your expenses consume more than 45% of your revenues?
___	___	Do you sometimes have trouble meeting monthly expenses?
___	___	Have you had to borrow to meet basic operating expenses within the last year?
___	___	Do you have less than six months' worth of operating expenses (including your compensation) set aside for emergencies?
___	___	Does it take longer than 60 days for your clients to pay you?
___	___	Do your accounts receivable equal more than two months' worth of revenues?
___	___	Is your realization rate lower than 90%?
___	___	Are you operating without a written business plan, budget, or marketing plan?
___	___	Do you write off direct client expenses incurred in-house (e.g., postage, fax, photocopies, phones, etc.)?
___	___	Are you without a plan to increase profitability over the next five years?
___	___	When you set your fees, was your first consideration what your competition charges?

___	___	Do you want to add staff or another attorney, upgrade your technology, or buy a building, but can't afford to?
___	___	Does it seem that you are working harder now than you were five years ago, but with less to show for it?
___	___	Do you want to make more money?

Every "yes" is a red flag indicating that you've got some work to do. In the following chapters, you will find guidance on these issues and many more. Put in the effort and your practice will reward you nicely!

3

THE 3-POINT FOUNDATION:
THE BASE OF A SUCCESSFUL PRACTICE

Whether or not you are involved in the construction industry, you know that the first step in building a house is not putting up walls or raising the roof. Rather, you must first level your building site and pour a strong foundation. That foundation has to support your house for many, many years to come. If the foundation fails, the house becomes unstable and may eventually collapse for lack of a solid footing.

As with the house, building a successful and satisfying law practice requires a solid foundation that will support it for many years, as well. Instead of cement, a successful law practice is built on a three-point foundation made up of a:

- business plan;
- marketing plan; and
- budget.

The reason is pretty simple, really. The business plan shows you where you're going and how you're going to get there. The marketing plan defines your ideal client and lays out the strategies the firm will follow to attract and retain clients. The budget shows the projected costs associated with providing your legal services, along with your projected revenues. None is indispensable. All three are vital management tools and critical to your business decision-making process. When you make decisions that are not consistent with your overall plan for your practice, you can end up making some costly mistakes and/or derailing the practice altogether.

So, let's take a look at this critical three-point foundation. What is it and how do you develop the component parts?

1. The business plan.

Think of the business plan as your success plan because it defines your idea of success and lays out how you will achieve it. The business plan serves as the road map for your practice and keeps you on track when tempting opportunities and attractive distractions present themselves. An objective and well-written business plan:

- lays out your vision for your practice;
- defines who you are and what you are selling;
- defines your goals, breaks them into short-term and long-term goals, and defines the steps you plan to take to reach your goals;
- identifies the strategies you will use to turn your ideas into actual business practices;
- identifies your target market and how you plan to reach potential clients;
- pinpoints your firm's strengths and weaknesses;
- identifies your competition;
- helps you to identify and take advantage of business opportunities for which you are (or can be) uniquely suited;
- gives you a way to measure your firm's success in meeting your goals; and
- serves as a vital guide when making business decisions.

The business plan also gives potential lenders a look into your future, and helps them to assess the viability of your long-term strategies. It demonstrates how you will run a profitable business—and how you will repay the lender. The plan shows that you have examined your marketplace, found a spot for yourself, and identified and resolved potential problems before they arise.

"The business plan is a necessity. If the person who wants to start a small business can't put a business plan together, he or she is in trouble," says Robert Krummer, Jr., Chairman of First Business Bank in Los Angeles.

If you don't anticipate requesting a loan from your local banker, don't be fooled into thinking you don't need a business plan. You absolutely still do.

Unless you are seeking a bank loan, your written business plan doesn't have to be elaborate to be effective. A simple business plan with realistic goals can be less daunting, and more manageable, than a complex business plan with many divisions and appendices.

Before you begin drafting your firm's business plan, spend some time thinking about your dream:

- Where do you want to go with your practice?

- Do you want to grow, and, if so, to be what?

- What do you want the practice to look like when you retire?

- What are your expectations of your practice?

Nothing stays the same forever, so even if you don't have plans to change your practice over time, it will happen, and you need to be prepared. How do you want this firm to evolve? What will your firm look like in 10 years?

Your business plan should include your firm's mission statement. This is a combination of your core values and the vision you have for your firm, distilled down into one or two meaningful sentences. It should encompass the essence of who you are and what you want to be.

Before you think this is a piece of cake, let me just say this: "To provide the highest quality legal services and to protect our clients' best interests at all times," or anything remotely resembling this, is <u>not</u> a mission statement. If you'll review your ethics rules, you'll find that you are required to do this if you want to practice law. Besides, probably 99 percent of the law firms in this country have this, or something similar, as a mission statement. Get your own statement—and make it unique to your firm!

Example:

We strive to provide a friendly, supportive, and respectful work environment that will enable our employees to continue to grow and will empower them to care for and serve our clients to the best of their abilities.

The mission statement sets the firm's course—and this law firm has obviously learned an important lesson—to have happy clients, you must have happy employees. This statement clearly lays out the firm's commitment to its employees, as well as its expectations of superior performance on behalf of the clients. Good strategy! Open every staff and attorney meeting with a reading of the mission statement. It should be posted on the wall in a place of prominence for all to see. Most importantly, it should be lived every day through your words and actions.

When drafting your business plan, it's important that you get in touch with what you are really selling—and it's not high-quality legal services. Do you think your clients are coming to you for your legal expertise, your outstanding reputation, or your exemplary track record? ***Wrong***. While your clients definitely want tangible results, they are also seeking the intangible—understanding, compassion, security, a shoulder to cry on, an ally, someone they can count on, a champion, and more. Smart attorneys understand what they are truly selling and make sure their clients find what they are looking for with them.

Once you've completed your business plan, you need to get chummy with it. Take it to lunch, take it on your firm retreat, pull it out at attorney meetings—use it as the management tool it is meant to be. Consult it before you make any business decisions, large or small. When dazzling opportunities (I call them "bright shiny objects") present themselves, revisit your business plan and ask yourself if what seems to be a godsend will actually take you closer to your goals, or away from them. Your business plan reflects your vision for your practice. Don't lose sight of that like Gene and his partner did a few years ago.

The value of a business plan.

I remember clearly when I met Gene. It was October 25, 2001, just a few short weeks after the horrific events of 9/11. I was presenting a CLE that included a segment on business plans. After explaining the purpose of a written business plan, mentioning that businesses with formalized business plans are, on average, 10-50 percent more profitable than businesses without, and laying out the basics of a small law firm plan, I was surprised when one of the attorneys in the class challenged me on the necessity of a business plan. She sat, with arms folded tightly across her chest, and said, "I've been in practice for 18 years, never had a business plan, and nothing you've said here convinces me I need one. What do you have to say to that?"

Before I could answer, another attorney in the room raised his hand and asked if he could respond to this woman. He introduced himself as Gene and began his story.

Gene's grandfather had founded the firm some 60 years earlier. It passed to Gene's father, who spent his entire legal career there. When he retired, it came to Gene. Since then Gene had taken on a partner, two associates, and several staff members. Gene and the others enjoyed a pleasant practice in a quiet suburb of a major city, providing their clients with superior service in the proud tradition of his father and grandfather before him.

In early summer 2001, a potential client, with a large and expensive case that would be the biggest matter to ever come into the firm, contacted the firm. As Gene put it, "My partner and I were blinded by the dollar signs. We thought we were headed for Easy Street with this case. We couldn't accept fast enough. Then, the trouble began."

Gene and his partner failed to consider that opposing counsel was the largest law firm in the region. The full meaning of the situation hit when the delivery truck arrived with boxes of interrogatories and requests for production. The big firm looked at Gene's four-attorney firm and decided to crush it under a mountain of paper, knowing full well that Gene's little firm couldn't begin to match the manpower of the larger firm.

But, wait—things get worse. Gene and his partner were flying to Hong Kong the following month for four weeks of depositions. As he put it, "This is too soon after 9/11. My family doesn't want me to fly. I don't want to fly or be gone for a month, nor does my partner. The other part of this is that we are leaving our firm in the hands of our two first-year associates for 30 days."

Gene explained they had been so dazzled by the promise of wheelbarrows full of money that they didn't think about what else a case like this would mean to the firm, to its employees, or to its other clients. He turned to the doubting woman attorney and said, "We had a business plan. We reviewed it frequently. It kept us from making some stupid mistakes over the years; but, we momentarily forgot who we are and who our old and valued clients are. We are flying halfway around the world, and leaving our most important clients in the hands of two inexperienced associates."

He went on to add, "It remains to be seen if our firm can survive this. All I can say is that Ann is right. Write out your business plan, review it regularly, and stick to your course. We didn't, and we're paying big time for our stupidity."

I don't know if Gene's story convinced the other attorney that she needed a business plan, but it's certainly a compelling argument in favor of formalizing your vision. I hope you'll learn from Gene's mistakes and get your road map down on paper. Take your business plan to lunch once a month—you'll find it is fascinating company. Review your vision, track where you are in your progress, and check how much you've grown since you first wrote out your dream. Tweak, as necessary, but make sure you aren't tweaking it just to allow you to chase after one of the aforementioned bright shiny objects. Life has a way of bringing all sorts of tempting opportunities our way, but you have to hold each one up to the test— *"Will this take me closer to my goals or away from them?"* If it's going to be a detour, or if it will take you off in another direction altogether, then it's not for you.

And, yes, Gene's firm did survive, but it was a long recovery and they lost several long-time clients over it. The good news is that the partners' commitment to their business plan is stronger than ever. They are consistently making great business decisions and seeing continued growth in the business, just as they had planned.

Designing your road map.

So, let's go back to the future. Think about your dream law firm. What would you like your present firm to become? Perhaps the following questions will help you complete your visual image:

- If your firm could be anything you want it to be, what would that look like?
- Where would you be located geographically? Branch offices?

- Where would your clients be located?
- How would you be communicating with your clients?
- Would you be providing your services in a virtual environment?
- How do you see that working?
- Who would be working with you? (e.g., a receptionist, two paralegals, three associate attorneys, etc.)
- What practice areas would your firm offer?
- How would you deliver your legal services or other products? (e.g., traditional attorney-client relationship, Internet-based practice, downloadable forms packages, educational programs, books, etc.)
- What role would your firm play in the local community?
- What would your firm be known for? What would you personally be known for?
- How much money would you be earning per year?
- What is your end goal for your firm?

Do you see how this works? Entrepreneurs aren't locked into tradition—they dream of what might be.

Now, let's take a look at some of the component parts you'll want to include in your business plan:

- Our firm's mission statement
- Our goals and objectives
- Our values statement
- Form of ownership/legal entity
- History of the firm
- What we want to be known for
- The practice areas and services we provide
- What we are really selling
- Our clients (who are they, where are they)
- Our advisors (who are they, what do they bring to the table)
- Firm partners
- Firm employees (in-house and outsourced)
- Job descriptions for all employees
- Compensation and benefits

- Allied firms and businesses
- Vendors/bankers
- Our competition (who are they, where are they, what is their market share, how do they attract clients, what services do they provide, what is their pricing strategy, what is their reputation in the local community)
- The need for our services
- The office location, features, accessibility, and appearance
- How our firm differs from others
- Our marketing strategy
- What we are starting with (equipment, software, client base, etc.)
- Capital investments we'll make in the next three years
- Our financial plan
- Our pricing strategy, our fees, our billing methods
- Insurance
- Additional training necessary to achieve our goals
- The attorney(s) emergency and extended absence plan
- Exit strategy for the owner/partners
- What the firm will look like in five years
- The steps necessary to make the five-year goal a reality

2. The marketing plan.

Remember the movie *Field of Dreams*? Build it and they will come. That may work in the movies, but it's an entirely different story when you open a law practice.

Unless you brought clients with you to your new practice, chances are slim that you started out with a flood of clients clamoring to get through your front door. More than likely, your experience was (or will be) similar to mine when I started my business many years ago. Suffice it to say, we were not an instant success. We waited for the calls, but they didn't come. Why? Not enough people knew about us.

Marketing to bring in new business is a daily fact of life for small firm practitioners. While some attorneys view the whole idea of marketing as onerous, unpleasant, and, at times, a tad bit sleazy, it must be done. The trick is to develop marketing strategies that are effective and which you will actually get behind and implement.

For many solo and small firm practitioners, marketing dollars and marketing time are precious commodities. While most attorneys recognize the need to develop a marketing plan for their practices, I see many making poor decisions in choosing where to focus their money and efforts. Let's take a look at the marketing strategies used to market professional services; then, you'll be better able to decide which ones make the most sense for your practice.

In her book *Get Clients Now!,* author C.J. Hayden tells us that there are six proven strategies for marketing professional services:

- *Direct contact and follow-up*—Personal contact with a potential client, then following up with an e-mail or handwritten note. [NOTE: Check your local rules of ethics to determine what you can and cannot do with regard to direct contact.]

- *Networking and referral source building*—Building your business by helping others build theirs. Sharing information, contacts, resources, and referring business to each other.

- *Public speaking*—Speaking in front of an audience, either as a main presenter, a panel member, or the emcee who introduces other speakers.

- *Writing and publicity*—Writing articles for publication, blogging, newsletters, or getting written about or quoted in media stories.

- *Promotional events*—Presenting workshops for your target market or referral sources, co-sponsoring events, donating prizes to an event, sponsoring a Little League team.

- *Advertising*—Print ads in publications, TV or radio spots, Yellow Pages ads, websites, and direct mail.

The interesting thing about the six strategies is that I've listed them in order of effectiveness. Are you surprised to see advertising at the bottom of the list? You shouldn't be. Advertising puts your name out there, but generates lots of prospects, shoppers, and lookie-loos, with the occasional client mixed in. The first three strategies allow you to make a personal connection, which is far more powerful than just getting your name in front of people, as is the case with advertising. This doesn't mean that you shouldn't advertise; it simply points out the necessity of employing a variety of strategies to generate new business.

No like — no hire!

Marketers discovered long ago that we buy from those we know, like and trust. Think back to when you bought your house, your car, or an appliance. How did you feel about the salesperson? Chances are, you found the salesperson's personality agreeable and you trusted what you were told about the product. Would you have made the same purchase based solely on an ad in a newspaper or a radio spot? No, that would have attracted you, but it was the know-like-trust factor that sold you. It's only possible to develop that factor through actual contact.

With a referral, you benefit from reflected glory. The referral knows, likes, and trusts the person who referred him, so you're halfway home when he walks through your door. All you have to do is show him that the referral source was right in recommending you.

As someone who has done a lot of public speaking, let me tell you that the know-like-trust factor is huge if you do a good job in front of an audience. People may be a little shy, or even standoffish, with me before I speak; but, when I'm done, all of a sudden I'm on a first-name basis with everyone in that room. They line up with smiling faces and lots of questions. They send me thank-you notes, tell others about me, share my handouts with colleagues—and call to ask about my services. From hearing me speak, they know something about me, they may think they like me, and they trust what I'm saying.

The point is this: you need to incorporate a variety of strategies into your marketing plan for maximum effect. Direct contact, networking/referral source building, and public speaking are active strategies—you are personally involved and people have a chance to get to know-like-trust you. Writing/publicity, promotional events (other than workshops), and advertising are passive—people see your name, but they don't know anything about you. And, unless they see your name over and over, they aren't quite so likely to think of you if they have a legal problem. Passive marketing is more about being in the right place at the right time and getting your name in front of someone at the precise moment they need you. It's always good to get your name out there, but you need to be marketing through other strategies, as well.

Define your target market.

Before you can effectively market your services, you need to define your target market (made up of lots and lots of your ideal clients). [See chapter 6 on "Case and Client Selection" for help with developing your Ideal Client Profile.] Then, you must understand how your ideal client would shop for legal services. As an example, if you are a family law practitioner who handles high-end divorces, your clients will most likely not come to you from an ad in the Yellow Pages. These folks ask for referrals from their friends or other professional service providers. If you are representing baby boomers filing a Chapter 7 bankruptcy, your potential clients are less likely to ask for a referral because of embarrassment about their financial situation. Yellow Pages ads or a website might be good sources of new clients.

A savvy criminal defense attorney specializes in representing young men, ages 18-25, who have been charged with a criminal offense. The attorney's best marketing tools are Facebook and YouTube because he knows that's how his clients are accustomed to communicating with each other. Put your effort and money into trying to reach your client in the most effective and direct manner.

Attorney, know thy client.

Budget for marketing—time and money.

The next step in crafting your marketing plan is budgeting money for marketing activities. Decide how much money you can allocate to marketing efforts (typically 2-5 percent of revenues) before you choose your strategies. As an example, if you've only got $100 a month to spend on marketing, you aren't going to be able to do big Yellow Pages ads. Because advertising is the least effective marketing strategy for professional services, spend your limited funds on a strategy that has a higher expected return on investment (e.g., networking and referral source building or public speaking).

In addition to money, you need to budget time for marketing activities. As an example, if you budget five hours per week, that might include one local bar luncheon meeting, 30 minutes twice a week writing handwritten notes to referral sources or people you admire, plus one coffee date and an after-hours Chamber of Commerce mixer. Five hours per week is a reasonable amount of time for marketing. Marketing activities are not always one-on-one meetings. Give yourself credit for having lunch with a fellow CLE participant, adding content to your website, searching out organizations for possible speaking engagements, working on your newsletter, working with a graphic designer on new business cards, etc. Commit to a specific amount of time per week and then find ways to productively use that time.

Now, let's put together a simple marketing plan for your practice.

MY MARKETING PLAN

The firm's mission statement:

_____

_____

_____

Our core values:

_____

_____

_____

The things we do really well are:

_____

_____

_____

The things we need to work on are:

_____

_____

_____

My target market is:

_____

_____

Within my target market, my ideal client is:

_____

_____

My goal for my marketing plan this month is to _____
(e.g., add three new clients, increase visibility, add five new referral sources, get two speaking engagements, get my name in a media story).

Using the six proven strategies, my chosen activities under each strategy are:

Direct contact/follow-up

_____

_____

_____

_____

_____

_____

I will do this _____ times this week/month.

Networking/referral source building

_____

_____

_____

_____

_____

_____

I will do this _____ times this week/month.

Public speaking

_____

_____

_____

_____

_____

I will do this _____ times this week/month.

Writing/publicity

_____

_____

_____

_____

_____

_____

I will do this _____ times this week/month.

Promotional events

_____

_____

_____

_____

_____

_____

I will do this _____ times this week/month.

Advertising

_____

_____

_____

_____

_____

_____

I will do this _____ times this week/month.

3. The budget.

With your business plan in place and your marketing plan fleshed out, it's time to figure out how much money you're going to need to implement these plans and operate your practice. We do this with the help of a handy-dandy little management tool called a budget.

Actually, you don't need *a* budget—you need multiple budgets—all of which are important management tools. Specifically, the three must haves are:

- Operating budget (projections of the various costs and expenses associated with operating your business)
- Income budget (projections of anticipated revenues)
- Capital expenditures budget (projections for the purchase price of assets whose return is expected to occur over a period of time).

Let's look at what you might include in these three budgets, beginning with the operating budget. If you don't already have an operating budget, start by reviewing your profit and loss statements for the last three years. You'll get an idea of trends and annual increases that need to be factored into your budget.

If you have a bookkeeper, that person can help you develop your budget. If you do your own books, then look to your software to help you with this task. A simple budget can be crafted from the line items on your profit and loss statement. As an example, let's look at some of the expenses you might expect to see in your operating budget:

SAMPLE OPERATING BUDGET

Projected overhead expenses

Advertising	
Website hosting/maintenance	
SEO consulting	
Ad in PAWS fundraiser program	
Miscellaneous	
Professional fees	
CPA	
Ann Guinn, Practice Management Consultant	
IT consultant	
Contract labor	
Contract attorney	
Virtual paralegal	
Virtual legal assistant	
Education and seminars	
Employee expenses	
Payroll	
Employer expenses (payroll taxes, etc.)	
Benefits (including health insurance, retirement plan contributions, etc.)	
Gifts	
Insurance	
Professional liability	
Owner medical/dental	
Owner life	
Business interruption	
Renter's insurance	

Marketing/business development	
Rent	
Office	
Equipment	
Depreciation	
Interest (other than mortgage)	
Meals and entertainment	
Mortgage interest	
Office expenses	
Online research and library	
Parking	
Finance charges	
Bank service charges	
Merchant account fees	
Late fees	
Miscellaneous office expenses	
Postage and delivery	
Repairs and maintenance	
Supplies	
Kitchen	
Office	
Taxes	
Licenses and permits	
Travel	
Utilities	
Charitable contributions	
Dues and subscriptions	
TOTAL	

SAMPLE INCOME BUDGET

Revenues generated from all of your income streams

Professional fees	
Legal services	
Consulting services	
Book sales	
On-line	
Bookstores	
Back-of-the-room sales	
Downloadable forms	
Public speaking	
Guest speaker fees	
Continuing education programs	
Instructor's fees	
Law school	
Community college	
Other	
Workshop registrations	
Promotional public programs	
Client-oriented programs	
Notarial services for other businesses/public	
Rent from subtenants	
Other	
TOTAL	

CAPITAL EXPENDITURES BUDGET

Investments in the business

Real property purchase	
Office building	
Parking garage	
Vacant land	
Hardware/equipment	
Computers	
Printers	
Scanners	
Photocopiers	
Other	
Office premises	
Remodel	
Build-out	
Addition	
Office furnishings	
Furniture	
Artwork	
TOTAL	

When all is said and done, the three-point foundation: a business plan, a marketing plan, and a budget, is critical to your ability to proactively manage your practice. Spend as much time as necessary to craft these documents in such a way as to provide guidance as you make both short-term and long-term decisions. Properly prepared and followed, they will help you stay the course, save time and money, and help you avoid making costly mistakes. That's what I call a good return on investment!

> *Tip: The three-point foundation: without it, you're liable to find that your business is built on sand!*

4

MAKE A NAME FOR YOURSELF:
FOCUS YOUR PRACTICE

When your great-grandfather opened his law practice, lawyers were like the old general practice doctors; they handled anything and everything that came along. Need a will? I can do it. Got cheated on a horse swap? I'll take care of it for you. Want to stake a claim to a section of the river that you think holds the Mother Lode? No problem, I'm on it. You've got an idea for a new ramrod to help you load your rifle? Step right this way to apply for a patent. Want to buy the old Hackelman place? It's as good as yours.

Times have changed and so have clients' needs. The simplicity of the law was lost many years ago, and in its place is a monstrous tangle of ordinances, regulations, and laws covering everything from who gets Grandma's china when she didn't leave a will to which country has rights to a pod of orca whales frolicking in the Pacific Ocean. It's too much and a single attorney cannot possibly know it all. So, if you're trying to be all things to all people — give it up.

Going back to the doctor analogy, think of it this way. You awaken one morning with a severe pain down your left arm, dizziness, chest pains, and shortness of breath. Quick, who do you call—a general practitioner or a cardiologist? You aren't sure what's wrong, but wouldn't you feel a whole lot better having someone who deals with these symptoms all the time checking you over? Someone who knows when chest pains are heart-related and when they are the result of indigestion? Someone who knows exactly what to prescribe and the correct dose for your age and body size? Someone who knows the right questions to ask and what to do with your answers?

Law firm clients feel more comfortable dealing with someone they perceive to be an expert.

Clients feel the same way about attorneys as you do about a doctor treating your chest pains—they want someone who has been down this road before and knows what to do. They understand that an experienced attorney has a high level of expertise, and because of that, the practitioner can do the work much more quickly than someone who is learning as he goes. The faster the work is done, the less it will cost. Clients don't like paying for an attorney's learning curve.

Even with the complexity of the current laws, many small firm attorneys still tend to handle multiple practice areas so they don't lose any potential clients. This puts a lot of stress on the attorneys, and could jeopardize the client through faulty, but well-intentioned work.

Focus with a purpose.

Focus your law practice on one or two practice areas that are complementary, thus allowing for cross-selling of your services. An example would be adding estate planning to a family law practice. Everyone who goes through a divorce needs a new estate plan. Why refer that work away when you could do it yourself? How about family law paired with criminal defense for matters of domestic violence.

Why focus your practice? It's pretty simple; you'll:

- earn 10-15 percent more than generalists, on average;

- become more efficient with your work, and that leads to increased productivity and profitability;

- increase referrals by building a reputation. You are much more likely to become known for your expert knowledge in a particular practice area than for your general knowledge of multiple practice areas. When you and your fellow attorneys talk about the experts in your field, how many times does the name of a general practitioner get mentioned first? Would you rush to sign up for a CLE on the new Social Security laws if it was taught by an attorney who handles family law, bankruptcy, personal injury and criminal defense in addition to helping an occasional client with a Social Security issue? How likely are you to refer a client to a generalist over a specialist?;

- attract high caliber talent who want to work with you;

- reduce or eliminate your competition;

- be able to increase your rates above your competitors;

- save CLE dollars because you won't need to take programs in multiple practice areas; and

- save marketing dollars because you'll know exactly who to market to and how to reach them in the most effective manner.

Other than that, I can't think of a reason to focus your practice. Now, for the sake of fairness, I am perfectly prepared to hear your reasons for not focusing your practice. Okay, we both know I can't hear you, but I have heard plenty of other attorneys try to convince me that listing five separate practice areas on their business cards makes sense—and I have yet to buy into one of their explanations.

What it means to focus.

So, let's look at what it means to focus your practice. *Focus* doesn't necessarily mean you have only one practice area; rather, it can refer to *a practice that meets the needs of a particular segment of the market.* For instance, if you want to focus on the needs of business start-ups, that could encompass entity formation, policy manuals, employment issues, IPOs, copyright and trademark work, patent applications and defense, real estate development, and more. You see the focus here is on helping new businesses with all of their legal needs, not just incorporation. That's what I mean about complementary practice areas; they help you provide fuller service to your clients to meet their needs. You've also got a built-in channel for new work as your clients grow their businesses.

Another example is family law. I've never understood why family law refers primarily to dissolutions. If you were a true family law attorney, you would be serving the needs of the greater family. That could include estate planning, probate, Medicaid issues, adoptions, nursing home abuse, guardianships and conservatorships, end-of-life issues, and so on. You could even throw in personal injury because that certainly is a family issue in many cases.

A relatively new practice area is animal law. I think of dog-bite cases when I think of animal law, but an animal law attorney may also handle purchase/sell agreements for race horses, importation of animals from other countries, sale of livestock across state lines, animal abuse, injury or death of an animal caused by the negligence of a paid caretaker, or injury caused by an animal.

It's so much easier to market your practice when you are known for something. One of my clients is well on her way to becoming known as "*the* trademark attorney for green businesses." She lives and breathes green. She donates a portion of her earnings to environmentally conscious groups. Her office and home are 100 percent wind powered. She sends me thank-you notes on beautiful biodegradable note cards that are impregnated with wildflower seeds. The instructions on the back tell me to plant the card in a pot, add water, and watch for the miracle to happen. She goes to every conference, trade show, and forum in this burgeoning industry. She serves on the boards of several environmentally friendly nonprofit organizations. She knows exactly who to market to and how to do it because her practice has such a sharp focus. She spends no money on Yellow Pages ads. When she networks, it's with targeted people in specific settings. In all my years, I've never seen a more focused practice. You cannot separate her personal commitment to sustainability from her law practice. They are one and the same. In just a few short years, she has built a name for herself, and it's not one that you would recognize. But, her potential clients know her—and that's what counts.

How to focus.

To figure out what new services you might add, you first need to know if there is a need for these services. Solicit information from your local chamber of commerce on the demographics of your community. Read the local business journal and the business section of your newspaper. Find out what businesses are coming in, then think in terms of what that could mean to your practice. As an example, a new data center is being built on the edge of town. What does that mean for attorneys? Employment, real estate, pension plan, land-use, construction, housing, and easement issues are a few of the practice areas that could be needed.

Watch for trends in segments of the population. Is your community growing because of an influx of senior citizens looking for affordable living? That will mean senior housing and independent, assisted living, and skilled nursing facilities will probably come in, as well. Estate planning and probate work could pick up. Pension plan issues and securities litigation could increase.

Let's say you pick up the paper tomorrow morning and find that a local manufacturer is laying off 370 people. What legal issues might arise there? Wrongful termination, pension-plan collapse, age discrimination, retaliatory treatment, and unemployment benefits issues are among the many that come immediately to mind.

There is opportunity all around you, in any economy. The key is to recognize it and incorporate it into your business plan. Develop a focus to your practice and become known as *the* attorney to go to for specific issues. Your clients will appreciate working with someone who specializes in particular problems because you're going to save them time and money, and they just might end up with a better resolution because of your heightened expertise. And, they'll love bragging to others that they went to the best attorney in town for their problem!

> *Tip: Sharpen your focus and you'll find yourself standing out from the crowd!*

5

MARKETING SMARTS:
HOW TO ATTRACT THE RIGHT CLIENTS

Okay, you've graduated law school, passed the bar exam, and set up practice in a solo or small firm. You have an ad in the local newspaper, you have a one-page website, and your business cards sport four colors. All you have to do now is stand aside to avoid injury as your eager, clients-to-be come rushing to your door, right? I heard of that very thing happening once. Oh, wait, that was Starbucks. Sorry, my mistake. I've never actually heard of that happening in a law firm.

What's more likely to happen if you adopt a build-it-and-they-will-come attitude is that you'll have sufficient time to get really good at computer games, satisfy your mother's seemingly never-ending need for check-in phone calls, and organize and reorganize the business card you received from the building manager when you moved in—and then your business will fold and you'll need to spend your free time looking for a job.

Perhaps my personal story will help you avoid making the same mistakes my business partner and I made when we started our business. Bear with me, it has a happy ending.

When Deanna and I decided to go into business for ourselves, we did six months of heavy research. We interviewed successful entrepreneurs, took classes, read books, and developed our business plan. Everything we read, and everyone we talked to, offered the same advice: don't quit your day job until you have your first client. Too bad we didn't listen. Instead, we told a few law firm administrators, whom we knew, about our new business. Everyone was quite encouraging and we interpreted their kind words as acknowledgment of the brilliance of our business idea. So, we got a phone line installed in my second bedroom, had some cards printed up, signed up for all the new credit cards we could get while we still had steady income, and quit our jobs.

During our first month in business, we had exactly three phone calls—two were from my mother, checking to make sure our phone worked.

We thought we were offering a service that all large firms needed, and all we had to do was sit back and wait for our administrator friends to call. In hindsight, I realize how stupid we were. Deanna prefers the word "naïve." Whatever you call it, we had no business—and worse, no idea how to get any business.

At Christmas that year, my dad said to me, "You've been in business for six months. How's it been going for you?"

I gamely replied, "Well, in the first six months, I've grossed $148 and I hope to double that next year."

It wasn't until we had pretty well exhausted the cash advances on all of our new credit cards that we got serious about undertaking some marketing to bring in business. While we were far from an overnight success, our marketing efforts paid off and we started to attract clients. Although Deanna went on to other things many years ago, I'm proud (and more than a little stunned) to say that my business celebrated its 23rd anniversary in 2009. And, despite being in business for 23 years, actively marketing my services is as important today as it was in 1986 when we were trying desperately to attract our first client. My marketing learning curve was and is significant. (I say, "is" because I think there is no end to what you can learn about marketing.) Life might have turned out differently for us if we had known both *who* to market to, as well as *how* to market our services, in those early days. It also would have helped if we had been clear on *what* our services were, and, thus, what we were marketing.

What exactly is marketing?

In developing your marketing plan, you first need to understand what the term "marketing" means. Every marketing expert has his or her own definition of the word:

"Marketing is telling people what you do, over and over and over again."

"Marketing is the outward demonstration of who you are and what you do."

"Marketing is what you do to attract clients."

"Marketing is advertising and beyond."

Actually, marketing is all of the above, and more. Marketing is about:

• your image;

• your message;

- your brand;

- the quality and timeliness of your work product;

- how you treat your clients;

- how you treat others;

- how you manage your staff; and

- keeping promises and following through.

One of my clients summed it all up by stating, "Marketing is everything you do." I would add, ". . . and everything you don't do." This is truly a case of actions speaking louder than words. Failure to treat people well, take action as promised, or return phone calls in a timely manner is marketing, too, although, usually unintentional marketing (i.e., you don't think of your day-to-day actions as part of your marketing strategy). Frequently, your unintentional marketing is far more powerful than a high-priced newspaper ad or a flashy website. Make sure your unintentional marketing message doesn't counteract the message of your intentional marketing.

Where are you on marketing?

If you are in business, you are doing some sort of marketing now, but is it working for you? Take a minute to answer the following questions to help you assess how much you really know about your firm's marketing strategies:

- How did you learn how to market your practice?

- Where do you get your marketing ideas?

- What is your marketing goal?

- Describe your current marketing strategy.

- How's that working for you?

- What are you doing now that is working really well?

- What are you doing now that isn't working so well for you?

- What have you tried in the past and discontinued? Why?

- How do you measure the success of your various marketing strategies?

- Which strategy is providing the highest return on investment?

- Which strategy is generating the highest number of your ideal clients?

- Describe a marketing campaign that has caught your attention recently. Why?

- Do you feel fear around marketing? What do you fear?

If you don't know the answer to some of these questions, chances are you've not taken the time to map out your overall marketing goals, or the strategies that will help you reach those goals.

Marketing is all about attracting new business, right?

Wrong! Most marketing plans are designed to attract potential clients; however, retaining happy, satisfied clients requires marketing, as well. That means you are marketing to your clients before you meet them, and then you continue to market to them after you are hired. You actually have four contact points—opportunities, really—when you market to your clients:

1. *Pre-hire:* marketing to attract potential clients to you.

2. *Initial consultation:* marketing to demonstrate to potential clients that you are the best attorney for the job.

3. *During representation:* marketing that continually demonstrates the value of your services to your client and the client's value to you, and reminds them why you were the best choice.

4. *After representation:* marketing that helps keep you top of mind with former clients for additional work or referrals.

Creating a marketing plan that includes attraction marketing, as well as retention marketing, will help you achieve the long-term results you want for your practice. Marketing experts tell us that it costs 11 times more to generate $1.00 from a new client than from an existing client. Plus, it's just plain more work to be continually marketing to draw in new clients. Save some money and use a portion of your marketing time to good advantage with your current and former clients.

Make sure every one of your clients knows *all* you do, and the many ways you can help them. Perhaps you can identify with my client Ted's experience. Ted was in the hallway outside a courtroom one day, waiting for a client's DUI hearing, when he spotted a former client coming out of the courtroom next door. Ted had represented the client on her own DUI matter a year or so earlier. He approached the client with a big smile and said, "What are you doing here today?" She said, "I just got a divorce." Ted was stunned, his two practice areas were criminal defense and family law. He blurted out, "Why didn't you call me? I do family law, too." The client looked confused and said, "I thought you only handled DUIs and traffic violations."

Ted made a costly mistake by assuming that his client knew all the services he offered. When we talked about it later, he came to realize that he had no firm brochure, his business cards didn't list his practice areas, and there was no lobby literature that would have alerted his clients to the variety of services offered. As he thought back, he couldn't remember telling her—or any of his other clients— about his other practice areas. That was Ted's fault. Discuss your practice areas during your initial consultation, mention them again during representation, and make sure that all of your follow-up contact with your former clients reminds them of your various services.

Become a resource for your clients so they call you first with a need. If you can provide the services they need, great. But if the issue is outside your area, giving a solid referral is the next best thing. The bottom line is that you've helped your client with a problem, and that's what the client will remember.

First impressions mean everything.

Let's start at the beginning. For the moment, we'll assume that you have plenty of potential clients calling the firm, so we know your pre-hire marketing is working for you. That takes us to the next level of your marketing, the initial consultation. Your potential client's experience with your firm doesn't begin with the first meeting, it begins with the first phone call. How satisfactory is your potential client's first encounter with your firm? Give your practice a quick self-audit on phone skills:

- How is your phone answered? Is the voice warm and welcoming?
- Who answers the phone? Does this person enunciate clearly? Possess good verbal communication skills?
- Does the person answering the phone work from a script geared toward potential clients? (The script should explain the services you provide, how you bill for your services, etc.)
- Does your employee address callers by title (e.g., Mr., Mrs., Ms., Dr.)?
- How many times does the phone ring before it is answered?
- Is the caller told how the initial consultation works (length of meeting, the fee, what to bring, what to expect from it)?
- Is your employee able to convert first-time callers into appointments?
- Is the caller given instructions on how to find your office, where to park, how early to arrive to complete the client intake form, etc?
- Do you follow up by mailing the potential client your intake form, a map to the office, your bio, the firm brochure, or any other helpful information?

If you want to know if your firm passes the smell test, ask two friends to call to inquire about your services and set up an appointment. [Two calls will give you a more accurate reading than just one.] If your firm doesn't come out so well, get busy and fix what's broken. Remember, the goal of that first-time call is to get the potential client in for a consultation so you can help them assess their legal issues and consider their options.

Okay, so you've got an appointment with a potential client on the calendar. Great! But, don't start counting your advance fee deposit yet–you haven't been hired.

The experts tell us that we form a first impression in the first six seconds of contact. What happens in the blink of an eye can take years to undo. Make sure that your potential clients have a terrific first six seconds!

To see what your clients see, try this little exercise I use with my clients. Walk out of your firm, stand in the hallway for a few minutes, then come back in, but with clients' eyes.

First, take a good look at your front door. How does it look? Is the firm's name clearly visible? Is the window clean? Is the door in good repair? Is the area outside your door vacuumed or swept clean daily?

Now, open your door and step through. Stop and take a good look around. What do you see? Boxes stacked in the hallway? A dead plant on a bookshelf? Stained coffee mugs on every flat surface? Clients' documents laying face up on the receptionist's counter?

Can you see into any of the private offices? Are they a mess? Can you overhear phone conversations?

How about those magazines? Do they reflect the interests of your clients or are they previously read publications from your home coffee table? Think about who your clients are and how they will view your choice of reading materials. A DUI attorney lost a potential client before they even met because of the magazines in his firm's waiting area. The table was piled with magazines from home, magazines about exotic travel and extreme sports adventure vacations. There was a publication for airplane owners, and another on luxury cars. The problem is his target market is the blue-collar Boeing machinist. His potential client took a gander at the magazines, and made a beeline for the door. On his way out, he told the startled receptionist that he didn't think he could afford this attorney. It was obvious to him that the practitioner was into pricey toys and entertainment. And, as the fleeing client surmised, "His clients are the ones who are paying for all that."

Who greets visitors to your suite? How long does it take for someone to acknowledge a visitor? Is the visitor offered a beverage? Styrofoam cup or ceramic? Is the seating in your waiting area comfortable and out of the flow of traffic? Is there artwork on the walls? Is it pleasing and restful to the eye? Is the wall color calming and peaceful?

Where do you meet with clients? What does that space look like? Is it clean and orderly? Is it a pleasant environment? Are there pads of paper and pens available for your clients' use? Are there remnants from your last client meeting strewn across the table or desk?

If you meet in your office, what does the client see as he or she enters the room? Files piled on the floor and sliding sideways on your desk? (That tells your potential clients how you will treat their files, as well.) Do you sit beside your client, or with a piece of furniture between you? Do you take phone calls while meeting with your clients?

The questions could go on and on, but you get the picture. Everything you do, everything your clients see, everything they experience in connection with your office—it's all part of your marketing. You owe it to yourself and your practice to step back and identify the marketing message you're sending out. If it's not the image you want, start making the changes necessary to convey the proper message about your firm to the world.

Your staff's part in your firm's marketing.

While you may be the key player in your office, your staff is sending out marketing messages, as well. Error-free work, appropriate attire, smiles, respectful forms of address, follow-through on commitments to clients, customer service, and phone manners all help to shape your clients' opinions of your firm.

Educate your staff on the importance of their behavior, work quality, and appearance as ambassadors of your firm. Ask your employees for their insight into what would help improve your firm's image. Ask them how they feel about working in your office. What do they tell their friends about your firm? Do their friends and family members know all the legal services you provide?

Help your employees develop their own elevator speeches (the 10-second introduction that describes what they do). As an example, "I'm Karen. I assist Adam Gwartz, a family law attorney, in helping clients through the difficult and stressful process of dissolving their marriages, or dealing with other personal family issues. I excel at providing the care and understanding our clients need during a critical time in their lives." Remember the know-like-trust factor that is the key to successful marketing? Could anyone *not* fall in love with Karen and her wonderfully warm and compassionate attitude?

Discuss marketing ideas in your regular staff meetings. Do some productive brainstorming by clarifying your goal for this session, and then ask everyone to throw out any ideas that come to mind (no critiquing until the end of the session). Next, select the most feasible and potentially effective suggestions. Assign responsibility for further information gathering or implementation, and set up a system of accountability to insure that progress is made.

The least expensive marketing tool is your business card.

Because the typical printed business card costs just pennies, you can afford to spread them far and wide. Everyone you meet should walk away with your business cards in hand.

Pass them out freely and frequently. Make it your goal to see how many business cards you can give away in a month—then, beat that record the next month, and the next.

Before you go skipping down Main Street, flinging your cards left and right with gay abandon, let's just make sure your business card is working for you. What's that you say? Your card looks just like the business cards of all your attorney friends? If that's the case, then "Houston, we have a problem."

As part of a class that I recently taught on networking skills for attorneys, the participants exchanged and critiqued each other's business cards. The ideas that came out of that session were invaluable and 100 percent of the class participants ordered new business cards by the time we met the following month. Here's an example of what they saw:

John Jordan
Attorney at Law

118 W. First Street	Albany, OR 97321
Phone: (503) 555-7800	Fax: (503) 555-7801
Email: john@jordanlaw.com	www.jordanlaw.com

A rather bland and uninteresting—but, typical—business card, don't you agree? What would you do to improve this card?

The first thing the group noticed is that the card doesn't mention what Mr. Jordan's practice areas are. They reasoned that anyone collecting a handful of cards at a local bar association meeting will have a hard time remembering Mr. Jordan's practice areas without prompting from his card. The group decided that a good business card tells what you do.

Second, the attorney group felt the scales of justice logo has been overused on attorneys' business cards. In addition, they felt that this logo doesn't mean anything at all to most young people. They suggested a different type of logo or graphic in an eye-catching color. The fax number was considered unnecessary in this age of e-mail. If someone needs to fax you, they can call for the number.

The attorneys liked the typeface, although they had mixed feelings about the script font for the attorney's name and title. While some said it was hard to read, they did like highlighting the most important information in a strong and distinctive type style.

The one thing the group overlooked is the prime piece of real estate on the back of a business card. That's the perfect place to list your practice areas, put a picture of your smiling face, give your website address in large letters, or put a couple of client testimonials. Optimize the value and effectiveness of your business card by using both the front and back of the card to promote your practice.

Be careful in your choice of graphics and logos. If your readers don't understand what they are seeing, your efforts are pointless. In our group exercise, one of the attorneys had a stylized "V" as her logo. She chose it because it's the first letter of her last name. Unfortunately, the other attorneys in the group thought it was a seagull and no one could figure out what a seagull had to do with her practice area (probate tax issues). The attorney wanted to be identified with an elegant "V", but in reality she was being linked to flying scavengers.

Design your card for your reader, not for you.

So, how can a card be made more useful? The following example shows some options for both the front and the back of the card:

Jordan Law Office
(503) 555-7800

John W. Jordan
Attorney at Law
Copyright and Trademark Law

118 W. First St   Albany, Oregon 97321
Email: john@jordanlaw.com

(Front of card)

For all of your copyright and trademark needs:

Applications
Licensing
Unauthorized Use
Infringement
Renewals

www.jordanlaw.com

(Back of card)

Some things to keep in mind in designing your business card:

- Make sure your name is easy to spot. That's the most important part of your business card.

- Leave lots of white space to give the eye a rest and to avoid overwhelming the reader.

- Leave off any extraneous information (e.g., your cell phone number, unless you really want clients, referral sources, and looky-loos calling you when you're at the park with your kids or lying on the beach in Cancun).

- Add some visual interest. A logo, graphic design, or color will help your card get noticed. In a pile of business cards, yours is more likely to be the first that will be picked up.

- Match your card's colors, logo, and graphic design to your firm stationery and website. Consistency of the visual elements of your firm helps to develop your brand.

- Stick with one font style and size for a uniform look. The exception would be if you choose to highlight your name in a distinctive typeface.

- Don't forget to use the back of your card.

Once you've designed your card, show the design to several friends and colleagues. Ask for suggestions on how to increase the effectiveness of the card. Ask the important questions:

- What's working and what isn't?

- Can you identify my practice areas?

- What does the card stock say to you?

- What about the colors?
- What message does the logo convey?
- Can you easily read the typeface?
- Does my name jump out at you?
- Is the layout pleasing to the eye?
- What is your overall reaction to the card?
- Based on this card, what impression have you formed of my firm and me?

Exchanging business cards is an art—do it with deliberation.

Once you've got your cards in hand, offer them to anyone and everyone, but, always ask first "May I give you my card?" Always pass your cards out in pairs: "Here's one for you and an extra one in case you have a friend who might need my services." If you've printed information on the back of the card, fan the cards out—one face up, one face down—so the recipient notices that there is information on the backside.

The trick to exchanging business cards is to get the other person to actually read the card and remember you. Is that possible, short of using brute force? Of course. Here's how.

For many years, I had business dealings with two Japanese companies, and I learned the art of exchanging business cards from my Japanese guests. Americans often have a rather off-handed way of exchanging business cards, but the Japanese treat a business card with the same respect they show the individual behind the card.

When the Japanese exchange *meishi* (name cards), all activity and conversation stops. The Japanese extend their card to you, holding the card by the upper corners with both hands, bowing as they do so. The print is properly positioned for reading. You don't exchange cards at the same time (American style). The recipient accepts the card with both hands—and then, actually *reads* it! The polite thing to do is to make a comment on the card. This was particularly challenging for me because many of the cards I received were printed in kanji, or Japanese characters. I hadn't a clue what the card said, but I knew I had to make a polite comment, so I developed a few little tricks that worked well. Usually, the city name was in English characters, so I would mention the city and ask its location. Sometimes it was obvious to me that there were several addresses listed, so I would guess that the business had multiple locations. That provided an opportunity to say something like, "Oh, a large company. Eight locations. Very successful." My guests were always pleased with my comments because I was demonstrating not only good manners, but an interest in them and their businesses, as well—a good tip when dealing with business cards in languages you cannot read.

If you adopt the Japanese manner of business card exchange (I'll leave the bowing part up to you), you'll be surprised at the reaction of most Americans. When you take time to read the card and comment appropriately, or ask a question, Americans tend to look surprised and inevitably reach into their own pockets and pull out your card to reciprocate the action. When you take time to really read a business card, you are helping yourself secure that individual's place in your memory bank. And if someone does the same with your card, you've also improved your chances of being remembered. This is a great way to further your conversation.

A business card is a handy thing to have around.

Like your American Express card, never leave home without your business cards. Keep a supply in your desk, in your car, in your briefcase, and at the receptionist's desk in your lobby. Use them to leave a note for someone. In a committee meeting, write a request or assign a task on the back of your card and pass it to the appropriate person. (Now the individual has a reminder of what he is to do, and your contact information to get back to you). Suggest to other professionals that you keep each other's business cards on display in your respective waiting areas. As an example, if you handle family law matters, you might arrange to have your cards on display in the office of a family counselor, and vice versa. A DUI attorney might work an exchange with an alcohol recovery counselor or a rehab facility. Choose someone who is likely to come in contact with your target market and offer the same in return.

Be creative. An estate-planning attorney attached his card to a bouquet of flowers that he sent to the nurses who had cared for his mother following surgery. One of the nurses called to thank him and to schedule an appointment to meet with the attorney to update her will.

Who is your best resource?

In our lives, we all know people whom I would describe as centers of influence. They are the folks who are at every meeting. They are the ones everyone calls when they need advice, a referral to another professional, or an introduction. They don't just belong to groups—they are actively involved, and highly visible in their groups. They are likable, friendly, and trustworthy. In short, they are a lot like you, except they seem to know everyone in the Western Hemisphere on a first-name basis. If you are not a center of influence yourself, then you need to further your friendship with someone who is.

Research indicates that we each know about 500 people well enough to pick up the phone and call and they would know who we are. Each of those people know 500 people; so, you can see that by getting your marketing message out to only 10 people, you have the potential of having your message reach 5,000 people. If you send your message to 500 people, your potential pool becomes 250,000!

Centers of influence know far more than 500 people. So, the fastest way to connect with the right person or people is through your center of influence. It works along the lines of the "Six Degrees of Separation" theory. That's the idea where you can meet anyone in the world by going through no more than six people. Sometimes, it takes far less than that.

Recently, one of my clients told me that he had a personal passion to promote research into a particular brain disorder that afflicts his daughter. He had his eye on billionaire Paul Allen, co-founder of Microsoft, because Mr. Allen's foundation has funded a great deal of research into mental health issues. My client said, "I'll be ready soon to present my idea to him, but in the meantime, I've got to figure out how in the world I could ever meet him. It's not like we hang out at the same pizza joint."

Several weeks later, I was using this illustration to promote the idea of personal passion in another law firm. When I concluded my comments, I said, "So, now he's looking for a way to personally meet Paul Allen. I told him that in his sphere of influence, he knows someone who knows someone who knows someone who could introduce him to Mr. Allen."

One of the attorneys in the room raised his hand and said, "I could. My roommate is a vice president in Paul Allen's charitable foundation."

See how it works? You know people who know the people you need to meet. They know potential clients, other professionals with whom you could form alliances, other referral sources, dentists, babysitters–you name it. You just need to ask for an introduction. People don't know how they can help you unless you tell them.

To start, grab a yellow pad and write down the first five names that come to mind. Don't think only of centers of influence or referral sources. That's not important right now. Just the first five names. Then, add five more names. Now, you've got a list of 10 people you know well because they were top of mind for you (you thought of them first). These 10 names are the start of your referral source list. Make it a goal every day to add names to your list. After you hang up from a call, write the caller's name on the list. Every time you come back from a bar association meeting, add the names of the attorneys with whom you spoke at the luncheon. When a client drops by, that name goes on the list.

Your list will never be complete—you keep meeting new people all the time! All of these folks should be on your e-mail list for newsletters, announcements, and other communiqués. When you hit 500, don't stop! You know more people. How about Muriel, your dry cleaner? Mike, at the pet store? Tamika, at your local coffee hangout? You get the picture. You know a lot of people, and each is a potential referral source for you. It's your job to make sure they know what you do and who your ideal client is, and that you would welcome their referrals.

Let's go back to your original 10 names. Look over this list and put an asterisk beside any name you deem to be a center of influence. Those are the folks you should be networking with most frequently. They are the ones who have the broadest ripple effect. They are the best-connected people, the individuals most likely to know someone who needs your services, or someone you should meet. Applying the Pareto Principle to networking, 80 percent of your referrals should come from 20 percent of your contacts. That's only possible through centers of influence.

Pick out your first center of influence and give a call to get on his or her lunch calendar. You pick up the tab and be prepared to ask for the introduction you need. If you want to speak in front of a specific group, ask for help with that. If you want to meet the mayor, ask for help in achieving that introduction. If you want to serve on a board of directors, ask for a recommendation. And, be prepared to reciprocate in some way. At the least, a handwritten thank-you note, at the most a helpful introduction to someone you know.

Networking is not all about you!

Networking, in its purest form, is not about you, it's about the other guy. You look for opportunities to help someone else build a business, and good things will come back to you. Think about it for a minute. Has there been a time in your life when someone has helped you in some significant way? How did you feel about that help? Didn't you have just a drop of indebtedness mixed in with your buckets of gratitude? When you were able, didn't you start looking for a way to pay back the kindness?

Everyone with a social conscience has an open account with the "Bank of Debt Obligation." Someone gives you an unexpected Christmas gift and you run right out to buy one for her (usually bigger and more expensive than the gift you received because you feel guilty for not having thought of this sooner). Your friend picks up the tab for your golf game and lunch, so you make sure to grab the bill the next time you are together. Your new neighbor brings over a cake as a "welcome to the neighborhood" gift – and you return the cake plate piled with cookies. That's how the Bank of Debt Obligation works. When someone does something nice for us, we look for a way to repay that generosity or thoughtful gesture.

So, next time you go to a Rotary meeting, don't follow the lead of the guy who grabs 25 business cards, then runs back to his office to start bombarding everyone with sales pitches in a variety of forms. Make it a point to connect with only one or two people—but, on a meaningful and memorable level. Have a real conversation. Ask about his business. Ask about her ideal client. Ask what they need help with. Ask who they need to meet. Follow through on any promises and keep in touch. Then, watch what happens next. For the most part, people don't like to feel beholden to others. While your offer of help was completely sincere, so is their sense of obligation. Most people aren't happy until the account in the Bank of Debt Obligation shows a zero balance, and you are the lucky creditor!

There's gold in them thar clients!

Applying Pareto's Principle once again, it would seem that 80 percent of your business should come from 20 percent of your clients—either through new work from current or former clients, or from referrals. Many attorneys mention that they get a number of referrals from past clients. That's terrific! But, just think how many more referrals you could be getting if you actually made an effort to market to former clients.

It doesn't take much to stay in touch with past clients. Newsletters, birthday cards, occasional phone calls, checking-in e-mails—all pretty simple, inexpensive, and effective in keeping your name top of mind.

Learn the importance of maintaining contact after representation ends from Angelo's experience. One day, Angelo, a real estate attorney, decided to skip out on work and take his kids to the county fair. As he was wandering the fairgrounds in search of the scone mobile, he bumped into a client he had represented a few years back in the sale of some farmland. The client was happy to see Angelo, and they had a nice chat in front of the bratwurst stand. As they were about to part, the client turned to Angelo and said, "By the way, it's really fortunate I ran into you. I have a land-use problem with a development project I've undertaken—some problems with zoning and county regs. Is that anything you'd be able to help me straighten out?" Would he? Of course! The client said, "Isn't that funny. I know you handle real estate sales, but I would never have thought of you for zoning issues if I hadn't run into you today."

Angelo didn't find it funny at all. Apparently, he hadn't sufficiently educated this client as to the full scope of the legal services he provides, either at the time of representation, or since then. The case generated more than $100,000 in legal fees for Angelo—fees that would have gone elsewhere had Angelo not met the client at the fair.

Remember that marketing is telling people what you do over and over again. Don't overlook the potential gold mine in your former clients. Add them to your referral source list, and invite a different former client to lunch each month. Get caught up on their lives and refresh their memories on what all you offer.

So, how do I know if my marketing strategies are working?

To help you assess the cost effectiveness and overall success of your marketing efforts, you need to be collecting certain valuable information. Many attorneys will ask new clients how they heard about the firm (either by a question on the client intake form or during the initial consultation), but they do nothing with that information. You need to corral it all in one place, and then review it on a monthly basis to tweak your marketing plan for maximum effectiveness.

The person who answers your phone should be asking (and writing down) how each first-time caller heard about the firm. The client intake form should ask again. The attorney should ask during the initial consultation, and record the information on a tracking log, rather than in her notes for the client file.

When you review this input, watch for trends. Have several new clients come from one referral source? One ad? The website? Figure out what's working best for you and make sure you keep priming that source. As an example, if you have an expensive ad in a local publication, but in the last six months, not one client mentioned your ad, it might be time to drop the ad and put your money to work somewhere else.

At the end of this chapter, I've provided you with a list of certain bits of information you might find helpful. You'll have your own ideas to add in, as well. The important thing is to make tracking the source of new clients a priority. You might be surprised to learn that your fancy commuter mug give-away hasn't generated a single new client, but your spouse's participation in the local PTA group has brought in four new clients in three months.

What makes you different?

When I ask attorneys to tell me what makes their firm different from other law firms, I usually hear things such as:

- We provide the highest-quality legal services.
- We really care about our clients.
- We are creative in our approach to problem solving.
- We get the job done.
- We are aggressive in our representation.
- We are compassionate.

The list goes on and on, but the sameness is there—not one of these statements makes them different from most other firms. You are required by the rules of professional conduct to act with diligence and integrity on behalf of your clients. You are required to provide the highest-quality legal services. I've met very few attorneys who don't care about their clients. Part of diligent representation is creative problem-solving. If you don't get the job done, you get sued for malpractice and/or disbarred! Mother Teresa set the standard for compassion, and unless you can top her, you are probably operating at pretty much the same level as other practitioners when it comes to compassion.

What I'm talking about is what really sets you apart from your competitors. Offering foreign language skills sets you apart. Bringing your experience as a carpenter during your college summer breaks to your work representing victims of construction site injuries sets you apart. Using your personal experience as an RN for 12 years to help your personal injury clients, or medical malpractice clients, makes you unique. Accepting evening or weekend appointments makes you different from most other firms. Practicing out of a motor home that travels around your county makes you easily recognizable and special.

Competitive advantage comes from being different in a way that is readily identifiable to your potential clients. If you can't figure out how you are truly different from other attorneys, then get busy and develop a difference. Your marketing dollars will have a far greater return on investment when you give people a reason to call you first.

Tip: Everything you do—and don't do—conveys a marketing message. Make sure you do everything to the best of your ability!

MY REFERRAL SOURCE LIST

1. _____

2. _____

3. _____

4. _____

5. _____

6. _____

7. _____

8. _____

9. _____

10. _____

[Mark each center of influence with an asterisk. This is the person that you'll want to contact first.]

YOUR INTERNAL CHECK-UP BEFORE YOU START YOUR EXTERNAL MARKETING

How does our firm differ from our competitors?

_____

_____

_____

If I were my competition, what would I do to beat us?

_____

_____

_____

What is the value we provide?

_____

_____

_____

What is the most cost-effective, feasible, efficient, and natural mode of communicating my marketing message to my target market?

_____

_____

_____

What do I want to tell people about our services?

_____

_____

_____

What has been our most effective marketing strategy?

_____

_____

_____

Who/what has been our best source of new clients?

_____

_____

_____

What role will each person in the firm play in our overall marketing plan?

_____

_____

_____

WHAT I NEED TO KNOW TO MEASURE THE SUCCESS
OF MY MARKETING STRATEGIES

In tracking the success of my marketing strategies, it will be helpful for me to know (check all that apply):

_____   How our first-time callers heard about the firm

_____   Number of first-time callers per week/month

_____   Number of first-time callers who are converted to initial consultations

_____   Number of initial consultations that convert to clients

_____   What type of matter/issues are involved

_____   The dollar value of each client's matter

_____   How closely each new client matches our ideal client profile

_____   How our best clients found the firm

_____   How many callers asked for or were given a referral to another attorney

_____   To whom were those callers referred

_____   Advance fee deposit received

_____   Timely monthly payments

_____   _____

_____   _____

_____   _____

_____   _____

6

WHEN BAD CLIENTS HAPPEN TO GOOD ATTORNEYS:
CASE AND CLIENT SELECTION

Good case and client selection skills are critical to both the attorney's enjoyment of the practice of law and his ability to get paid. When an attorney takes every case that comes through the door, there are bound to be problems. Sorting the good from the bad is a learned skill, and, if you have ever had a client from hell, maybe you could use a little refresher on spotting the red flags.

Recently, I learned a new phrase—*rent case*. This refers to a case that an attorney accepts only because the practice is short on money and the rent (or some other immediate expense) is due. Not necessarily the best criteria for accepting a case. Sometimes it's worth it, lots of times, it's not.

Red flags warn of potential danger.

If you've ever had a bad experience with a client, hindsight usually reveals the red flags that were warning you off. While you know to turn away a potential client if there is a serious conflict of interest, or the client's case is weak, there are definitely other reasons to turn down new work, as well. Some obvious red flags should be flying high if the client is:

- argumentative or combative with you;
- unable to understand what you're talking about;
- unwilling to accept your guidance;
- unreasonable in his expectations;
- unable to pay your fees and associated costs;

- intimidating or threatening to your staff;

- someone you don't like;

- untruthful with you; or

- in need of excessive hand-holding.

If you spot these or other red flags, it may be best to guide the client to a referral service or another attorney who is more appropriate for this client. Trust me, there will be other clients—clients with whom you will enjoy working and who will be able to pay for your services.

To understand the effectiveness of your current client selection practices, ask yourself the following questions:

- Who is my ideal client?

- What percentage of my current clients fit this description?

- Which of my clients do I dislike? Why?

- What red flags did I notice during the initial consultation with those clients?

- Why did I accept them?

- Have I had a satisfactory relationship with these clients?

- Was it worth it?

- If I had it to do over again, would I make the same choices?

- What have I learned from these experiences?

- What red flags will I definitely pay attention to next time?

The initial consultation serves several purposes: it gives you a chance to assess the potential client and his issues, and it allows your potential client to get to know you a bit and decide whether or not you are the correct choice to help. Each of you will develop a gut instinct about the other, and you should listen to what yours is telling you before deciding whether or not to accept this client.

Who is your ideal client?

One of the best tools you can use to help with client selection is an "Ideal Client Profile," a detailed description of the person or business with whom you would like to work. Spending time now writing down the attributes of your ideal client can save you from making mistakes in the future. Depending on your practice area, definition can come from such things as:

- gender;

- age range;

- geographic location;

- educational level;

- annual household income;

- assets (e.g., home, business, cars, portfolio, etc.);

- ability to pay your fees;

- likability;

- ability to understand what you are saying;

- ability to actively participate in the attorney-client relationship;

- reasonableness;

- credibility;

- honesty;

- verbal communication skills;

- legal issue(s) involved and complexity;

- prior offenses/convictions;

- type and/or size of the client business (measured by annual revenues, number of locations, number of employees, services provided or products manufactured, and so on);

- general health;

- emotional stability; and

- prior experience with attorneys and/or the legal process.

Once you have your profile fleshed out, use it to evaluate potential clients. If you stick to representing only those clients who most closely fit your Ideal Client Profile, you will reduce the risk of ending up with bad clients. You should also be a lot happier in your work because you'll have handpicked exactly the clients with whom you want to work.

Now that you know who it is you want as a client, you need to ask yourself a few important questions before you agree to represent the client:

- How do I feel about this client and this case?

- Will I be able to maintain respect for this client regardless of what I may learn during my representation?

- Who will win this case (from the judge's point of view)?

- Is this a case I want to take?

- Does this case make economic sense? Will my potential client come out with money—more money than he/she will owe me?

- Are my potential client's expectations reasonable? Do they match up with my expectations?

- Can this potential client pay the advance fee deposit or flat fee up front?

- Will the case impose an undue burden on my staff?

- Does my firm have the resources available to handle this case?

- How much of my time will this case take?

- Do I have the time and energy to meet the demands of this client and this case?

- Does the potential client have the financial fortitude to pay the bills and costs in a worst-case scenario?

- If the client doesn't have the money to pay the costs, am I in a position to advance the necessary costs so that justice is served?

- Is the potential client emotionally stable?

- How will the potential client's case affect my other clients' cases?

- How will my staff feel about this client? This case?

- Are there red flags?

- Is my need for money right now influencing my decision on this client?

[A big thank-you to Eric Fong, a terrific attorney in Port Orchard, WA who provided many of the questions on this list based on his own lessons learned.]

IF YOU HAVE DOUBTS – DECLINE. I've heard many an attorney bemoan having taken a particular client, but I don't recall ever hearing an attorney lament having turned down a case. By developing your Ideal Client Profile, learning to trust your gut instinct, and facing facts, you might just end up working with people you like on cases that you enjoy, and avoid the headaches associated with bad cases or bad clients.

Fire away.

Once in awhile, despite your best efforts, a problem client or case will slip through even the most stringent screening process. You'll spot the signs soon enough, and when you do, you need to fire the client. While there are points at which an attorney is prohibited from withdrawing from representation, you still have plenty of other opportunities to terminate the relationship. Ask any attorney who has ever fired a client and they'll tell you, "It felt really good, and I feel so much better."

An attorney once told me, "I never give up on a client. I won't desert a client, even if they aren't paying me."

Huh? If the client isn't paying your fees, it seems to me that the client has deserted you. Cut your losses and fire the client. If the client is difficult to deal with, untruthful or uncooperative, fire the client. If your client is rude or abusive to your staff, fire the client. If the client's expectations turn into unreasonable demands, fire the client. If the client is unresponsive to your phone calls or e-mails, fire the client. If the client pushes you to do something unethical, fire the client. If you think you can't give your client 100 percent because of your feelings toward him, fire the client. Regardless of your feelings, he deserves 100 percent.

Hold out for your ideal clients, and your staff will be much happier, less stressed, and more productive—and so will you. As a bonus, you may discover that you are also making more money. It's a win-win situation—you get to work with clients you actually enjoy, and your clients get an attorney who actually wants to work with them. Imagine that!

> *Tip: If you have doubts about a potential client, take a pass. There will be others—I promise!*

7

MAKE YOUR CLIENTS
FEEL IMPORTANT:
KEEP IT PERSONAL

The difference between a good legal technician and a good attorney is the ability to make the client feel important. A good technician may write a brilliant brief, offer a stirring argument in court, and ultimately win a large award for his client, but if the attorney doesn't make his client feel important, he may end up with an unhappy client.

"That's nuts!" you say. "Clients are only interested in winning."

Bar grievances and malpractice suits prove clients want more than a victory.

Consider this true story. A technically brilliant plaintiff's attorney was sued for malpractice four times in two years by clients whose cases he had won. Despite some rather large jury awards, the clients were angry that the attorney had not been responsive to their phone calls and e-mails. He spoke to them in a condescending manner during their meetings. In his own words, he dumbed down the explanation of his legal strategies, "You aren't attorneys, so you wouldn't understand." He never sent copies of documents unless the client called several times to request them. He had his secretary relay all messages to or from his clients, and was unavailable to answer any subsequent questions the clients might have. His clients saw him in person during the initial consultation, and then again at the trial, but rarely in between. Associate attorneys conducted all depositions. Big awards do not insure happy clients. This practitioner was strong on legal skills, but woefully lacking in people skills. While he truly did care about his clients, he demonstrated his care by throwing himself into the technical side of his representation. The unfortunate result was that his clients felt like nonentities—they didn't feel his care. They never saw his compassionate side. He seemed to go out of his way to avoid direct contact with them once they hired him. He never made his clients feel important.

Let's consider another attorney's story. A young attorney got four referrals from one client in three years' time. This might be remarkable on its own; however, what made it even more remarkable is that he had lost the referring client's case. Interestingly, despite the loss, his client was not dissatisfied with him. Quite the contrary. The attorney had clearly and consistently demonstrated his concern for his client's welfare throughout their time together. He picked up the phone and called the client just to see how she was doing. He involved the client at every critical decision-making point, broke into a big smile and offered a hearty handshake every time he met the client, took time to listen to her fears when they would overtake her, and got a little misty-eyed when the judge ruled against her. At their first meeting, he gave the client a folder to hold all of the copies of documents he would be sending her along the way. He added in a couple of sheets of blank paper and encouraged her to write down her questions and comments for him there, so that when they next spoke, she would remember what she wanted to ask or tell him. Even though it was a contingent case, the attorney prepared an accounting of all he had done on the case each month and that helped her understand the value to her of his various actions. He provided her with a map of the courthouse, and highlighted the courtroom where she was to meet him. The map included information on public parking in the area, as well as restaurants and coffee shops nearby. The attorney spent time explaining what would happen in the courtroom, who each of the principal players would be, and how she should comport herself in the presence of the judge and jury. In short, he held her by the hand and walked beside her through the legal process. He made her feel important and cared for—and she showed her appreciation by giving him the referrals. She knew he had done his very best for her.

Which is the better attorney? Hard to say who has better technical skills, but it doesn't take a rocket scientist to see which lawyer is better at communicating care, concern, and interest to the client.

Communication is the first step in keeping clients happy.

If you ask your state bar association to name the most frequent complaint received about attorneys, the odds are great that it would involve communication. Failure to return phone calls, failure to adequately communicate during representation, failure to keep the client informed, or a host of other communication failures are the reasons for a great number of the complaining calls received by bar associations across the country.

Research has shown that 60 percent of attorneys are actually introverts. Conversation is not their strong suit. Being an introvert is all about, well, the introvert. Communicating with clients is all about the clients. When you can learn to truly put your client first in all things, you'll enjoy much more satisfying relationships with those who hire you, and you'll run the risk of developing happier clients.

How to open up the communication lines.

Not sure how to start? Try asking yourself:

- What are my client's expectations of the outcome of this matter? Of me?
- What does my client need right now?
- How is my client feeling about her case? About me?
- What can I do to help reduce my client's stress?
- When did I last send my client an update on her case?
- What update can I provide my client today?
- When is the last time I called my client just to say "hi?"
- When is the last time I spoke with my client?
- When is the last time I communicated in any form with my client?
- What is my client's biggest fear?

"So, I'm an introvert. How am I supposed to handle all of this client communication stuff? I'm feeling uncomfortable already."

Relax, you're already doing a lot of things right. Are there more things you could be doing? Probably so.

1. ***Set the right tone in the initial consultation***—Make the client feel special with your attentiveness and good listening skills. Smile, nod to encourage him to continue speaking, treat her as you would if she were a guest in your home. Make eye contact.

Let me digress here for a moment with a story about a client of mine. Ferdie is a family law practitioner. When we met, his business wasn't going so well. He was getting people in for initial consultations, but then he was losing them. Ferdie was a good attorney with a good track record, but still, they weren't hiring him.

Our first meeting lasted about 90 minutes, during which time Ferdie never once looked directly at me. His eyes would dart around the room, or he would become engrossed with something on his computer screen, or he would carefully study the papers in front of him—he looked everywhere but at me. I couldn't help but think this was a big cause of his problem.

Our next meeting a week later started out exactly the same way. After about 10 minutes, I said, "Stop. You've hired me to help you get more business, and I would be remiss as your consultant if I didn't tell you what I see. When we met last week, you managed never to look at me even once in 1-1/2 hours. Today, you're doing the same thing. When people come to you for help, they are emotionally shattered—the dream has died, the happily-ever-after life they had envisioned is gone. The person who promised to love them always and never to leave them has rejected them. Then, they come to see an attorney and he never looks at them. More rejection. A confirmation of their plummeting self-esteem. What they need is to see someone across this desk who cares about them, who looks them in the eye and clearly understands what they are feeling. You need to be able to offer them that. They need to see the care and compassion in your eyes. I know it's there, but they can't see it if you don't look at them."

Ferdie looked at me— in the eye!— and said, "Yeah, I don't know why I do that. I guess I'm just shy. I can change." With that, he fixed me with a piercing stare and I'm not sure he ever even blinked for the next hour.

About a year later, the client who had referred Ferdie to me said, "I just can't get over the difference in Ferdie."

I asked what he had noticed.

"Well, for one thing, he looks you in the eye when he talks to you. He never used to do that and it always made me uncomfortable. I thought I had something stuck in my teeth or something. He also smiles more and he seems to pay more attention when you're talking to him. He used to fidget, but now he listens. It's amazing. I don't know what's gotten into him."

That's why they pay me the big bucks. Ferdie still isn't signing everyone who comes in, but his average has gone up significantly since he learned a few basic tips on how to make his clients feel special.

2.   *Communicate during representation by returning those phone calls promptly*— For years, I encouraged attorneys to return calls within two hours; then I met an attorney who returns all calls within 15 minutes, and he shared a compelling argument in favor of this policy. He tells the story of how his son, a new attorney, followed his dad's lead in returning all calls within 15 minutes. When the son's firm unexpectedly folded over the weekend, the junior practitioner (with one year's experience under his belt) was out of a job and scared silly about finding another. Within 24 hours, he had a call from one of his former firm's largest clients, asking him if he would take over their work. The young attorney was stunned and asked why they were specifically coming after him. The response was "Joe Smith, another client of your firm, told me that you always return phone calls within 15 minutes. That's the kind of responsiveness we want in an attorney. You just can't find that anywhere."

When I ask attorneys about their return-call policies, I like to put the shoe on the other foot. "Let's say that you notice blood seeping from one of your body parts that doesn't usually bleed. In a panic, you call your doctor for guidance on what to do. How long would you expect your doctor to take before calling you back?"

Fifteen minutes? Two hours? Twenty-four hours? Two weeks?

When a client has a legal problem, he may as well be bleeding from some body part because he's just as nervous, just as agitated, just as unsure of what to do, as you would be if you were bleeding unexpectedly. There is a certain arrogance in not returning phone calls in a timely manner that your clients pick up on. The delay tells the client that you believe other things are more important than his questions or concerns. You can't forget for a minute that each of your clients is your most important client. Return those phone calls promptly, and if you can't, then someone else should. Your legal assistant can call to explain your delay in calling, and to ask if there is anything he can do to help or if there is a message he can relay to you in the meantime.

A couple of years ago, an attorney told me a lovely story about an experience with a former client (from two years past). For some reason, for more than a week, this woman kept popping into the attorney's mind. Finally, he picked up the phone and called her. The elderly woman burst into tears and said that she had just been sitting there, wondering if anyone even knew she was alive—or cared. She was feeling totally alone in the world and then the phone rang. They had a nice chat and as they were hanging up, the woman thanked the attorney repeatedly for caring about her, even when he wasn't getting paid to. The attorney had tears in his eyes as he recounted the story to me. That's what I mean about making people feel important.

3. *Call your clients from time to time during representation*—Pass along updates, just check in, ask about their child's Little League team—keep them involved—and keep you involved with them. Send them copies of everything to do with their matters. Send along relevant news articles. Invite them to lunch (no charge for your time, of course).

4. *After representation, continue to maintain contact*—through newsletters, holiday greetings, cards and notes, information on other professionals, interesting information on your website.

5. *Become a resource for your clients*—Let them know all of the other ways you can help them. Do they need a financial planner? You happen to know a couple of them. Are they looking for a new house? Give them the phone number for the real estate agent who lives next door to you. Do they need a speaker for their Rotary Club meeting? Hey, you happen to do public speaking.

One of the greatest gifts we can give to another person is to make him feel important. What can you do today to make each of your clients feel like your # 1 VIP?

> *Tip: The difference between a good attorney and a great attorney is the ability to make clients feel important!*

8

THE PERCEPTION OF VALUE:
WHAT YOUR CLIENTS SEE

I don't know about you, but I love people watching. We humans are endlessly fascinating, full of surprises, and totally illogical at the oddest times. Sometimes our logic flies in the face of, well, logical thinking, particularly when it comes to the perception of value. That's what allows us to attribute value based on the information we are given. Case in point: what I call "the free kitty syndrome."

The perception of value.

One fine day, as I approached the front door of my local grocery store, I spotted a young entrepreneur with a box containing four darling kittens. There was a sign affixed to the front of the box that proclaimed, "FREE KITTENS." The youngster was holding a little furball out to everyone who ventured near—"Try a kitten on for size," he was imploring.

Being a cat lover, I stopped to watch for a minute. It was great fun observing people's reactions to his offer. It's hard to resist a kitten, so lots of people were trying a kitten on for size. They would pick it up, cuddle it to their cheek, pet it, and put it back in the box and walk off. Time after time after time. No takers for these precious little creatures.

When I came out of the store about 45 minutes later, I was surprised to see the young man still sitting on the sidewalk with the box of four kittens. I stopped to chat with him for a minute and he said that he had been there about three hours and, while many people stopped to play with the kitties, no one had taken a free kitty home yet. He was about to pack it in for the night. He said, "My Mom's going to kill me. I was supposed to get rid of 'em all."

The next day, I found I was out of cereal, so I made a quick trip to the same grocery store. There was the same young fellow, but he was picking up his empty box to leave. I was pleased that the kitties had apparently found homes, so I stopped to congratulate him.

"I see you had better luck today. Good for you," I said.

"Oh, it wasn't me. It was the sign," he replied. He held up a new sign that read "KITTENS ONLY $5." He said, "If I'd had twice as many kitties, I could have sold them all. People were almost grabbing 'em out of each other's hands."

Same kitties, same cute little salesman, same location. The only difference this time was that they were no longer free. You see, *when something is free, we don't place the same value on it as we do something for which we have paid*. Think about it. If you win a free ticket to a concert in a radio station give-away, but you have a bad day at work and you just don't feel like going, you don't go. But, if you had paid $85 out of your own pocket for that ticket, you would drag yourself to the theater, no matter what. It's the perception of value. Right or wrong, if there is a monetary value attached—even if the dollar amount is not commensurate with the true value of the object—we believe it is more valuable. (Remember the insane prices for Cabbage Patch dolls for sale on the Internet a few Christmases ago? And, who could forget puka shell necklaces, Beanie Babies, or pet rocks?)

A friend of mine uses phone cards for all of her long-distance calling. She said that she's really annoyed because she's got a couple dozen cards lying around with anywhere from one to four minutes' time (at 2.9 cents per minute) still available—not enough to actually use for a phone call, but still, she can't bring herself to throw them out because "they still have value." In her case, the value isn't even useable, but the perception of value is still there for her.

Law firm clients are cut from the same bolt of cloth as were the grocery store-kitty people. We all look for value in the purchases we make and the services we use. It's obvious those kittens were exactly the same product whether they were free or cost $5; what was different was the customer's perception of value. While the kittens apparently had no perceived value when they were offered free, they were considered a real bargain when they were offered at "only $5."

Helping your clients perceive value.

When a potential client comes to your office, how do you help them establish a perception of value for your services? I have a number of clients who used to offer free initial consultations, but who now charge for that first meeting. The amount charged isn't important; it's the "free kitty syndrome" all over again. When a client is charged a fee for the consultation, it puts importance on the appointment and helps the client place a value on the attorney's advice. What's really interesting is that these attorneys have all reported a drop in "shopping" clients who never hired them anyway. For the most part, they are now seeing clients who are seriously looking for an attorney, not just shopping for the lowest price. Most interesting of all is that because they are seeing a better quality, serious potential client, they're getting hired more frequently from their initial consultations. They aren't giving away so much free time to people who have no real interest in hiring them, and that's time they can spend doing work for people who are paying them.

The key to developing a perception of value is delivering value. Helping your client determine the value to him of your services begins at your first meeting. Start guiding your potential client's perception of value by thinking of your initial consultation in a different way. Change the name of this meeting, and focus on the benefit to the potential client. A family law attorney might call the meeting a "Dissolution Options Analysis" or a "Family Planning Conference." An estate planning attorney might go with "Personal Assets Protection Planning Conference," or "Lifetime Wealth Protection Analysis." A bankruptcy attorney might choose to offer a "Debt Relief Strategy Conference."

Give your potential clients something of value to take away from your meeting. Use forms to help you outline the issues involved and the possible strategies for dealing with those issues. Give your potential client a copy to take home and study. If the client is interviewing several attorneys, you will stand out from the others because of the extra value you've given. If the client does hire you on the spot, your take-away form will serve as a reminder to the client of the various options you discussed with him, and clearly demonstrates that the client is in the driver's seat and can choose the course of action with which he is most comfortable.

Maintaining the client's perception of value is your responsibility throughout representation. At every opportunity, build maximum value into your services, and make sure your client understands that value. *Perception of value* is not about smoke, mirrors, and deception; it's about shaping your client's experience by delivering quality and value consistently.

Your client's perception of value affects how they feel about your fees.

I first learned the lesson of the perception of value from an antiques dealer in Oakhurst, California, many years ago. After I identified myself as a fellow dealer, we started talking shop. I was lamenting the fact that sometimes a really great piece can sit on the shelf for a couple of years, while other less-interesting objects fly out of the shop in the blink of an eye. I was saying that my merchandise is rather quirky and the shoppers at my mall don't seem to appreciate these wonderful, one-of-a-kind objects.

She smiled and said, "Mark up the price."

I thought she hadn't understood me, so I said, "That doesn't make much sense. If it hasn't sold at a lower price in a year's time, it sure won't help to raise the price."

The kindly shopkeeper shared with me the story of an old radio that had been in her shop for over a year with no takers. Priced at $175, the radio belonged to one of her most valued dealers—her husband. She finally gave him an ultimatum: "Get that thing out of here or slash the price. It's been taking up valuable space for way too long."

His response made her laugh. "Mark it $245," he said. "If it hasn't sold in 30 days, I'll bring it home."

"Done!" she said. She'd teach him a good lesson.

About two days after she changed the price tag on the radio, a woman came into the store, went over to the radio, and then came rushing up to the counter.

"Oh, my goodness. I've been looking at that radio for the last few months and it was $175 all along. Now, it's $245. I want it. Do you think the dealer will take less?"

The stunned shopkeeper said, "I'll give him a call." After a quiet conversation on the phone, she reported to the anxious customer "the dealer is willing to come down 10 percent to $220." The customer was elated and whipped out her checkbook.

As I was staring at the shopowner in disbelief, she said, "So, you see, it's all about the perception of value. Sometimes you have to help your customer build in the value."

When I got home, I tried it on an unusual salesman's sample box of window sashes. It had been in my antiques mall space for more than a year at $145, even through 30 percent off sales. I changed the price to $195 and it was gone in a week. I tried it again with an ugly, old Victorian hat rack that my friend was trying to sell for $65. I said, "The price is too low. That's more than 100 years old, and not a common piece. Put a '1' in front of that 65." He said, "You're nuts. This has been sitting here for nearly a year and it hasn't sold." I repeated, "Put a '1' in front of that."

A week later, my friend called to tell me of a "frightening occurrence" at the antiques mall. In his words, "Someone got loose from the home and ran wild through the mall. Before they could stop him, he had purchased my antique Victorian hat rack for $165 and run out the door with his new treasure. The clerks were terrified because it was obvious he was crazy—paying $165 for something he could have bought last week for $65." Sarcasm aside, the dealer changed the customer's thinking about the piece when he upped the price.

The perception of value.

I never advocate raising rates just to be raising them. If you are going to charge more for your services than your competitors, you need to make sure you're worth the higher rates. Build in the perception of value for your clients. Give them indicators that clearly demonstrate your value. If you don't do it, I can guarantee that your clients won't do it for you. Don't believe me? Have you ever uttered the words, "Well, you get what you pay for" or "What did you expect for this price?"

"Free" can have a price.

One last story. A family law attorney conducted a free initial consultation with a woman who was seeking an attorney to handle her divorce. The attorney thought it odd that the woman seemed to be interested in talking about only one or two aspects of her case, but wrote it off as just nervousness at actually taking a step toward ending her marriage. The woman left without hiring the attorney, but the practitioner felt confident that she would soon return and gratefully sign her fee agreement.

A few weeks later, the attorney was having lunch with several other family law attorneys in her community. One of them mentioned a strange happening. Seems that when the attorney was in court the previous week, he had run into a woman who had availed herself of his free initial consultation about a month earlier. He remembered her because she only asked questions about one particular issue in a divorce proceeding. She left without hiring him. Several others in the group recounted similar experiences, and when her name was mentioned, they realized they had each given her a free initial consultation, with her focus being on only a specific part of the legal process in each interview.

"What was she doing at court?" they asked their companion.

"Representing herself in her divorce," he replied. "She was using the free information we all gave her to great advantage."

Whether it's negative or positive, your clients will develop their own perceptions of the value of your services. The good news is that you can influence that perception by providing high value to each of your clients every time.

> *Tip: Your clients' perception of value determines their level of satisfaction with your services.*

9

STANDING OUT IN THE CROWD:
HOW TO WOW YOUR CLIENTS

While business publications regularly report on the business world's increased commitment to a higher level of customer service, many of us would be hard-pressed to name more than a handful of businesses that actually provide superior customer service. Can you describe three examples of exceptional customer service that you have enjoyed in the last month? Me neither.

Do any of the following scenarios sound at all familiar? Maybe your recent call to the phone company? You know, the time you called and heard, "Thank you for calling Phones R Us, Service Isn't, Telephone Company. In an effort to serve you better, please make your selection from the following menu. Press 1 if you understand you will never speak with a living person in our company. Press 2 if you have all day to wait while we try to get our repairman to your office sometime between 8:00 a.m. and 5:00 p.m. a week from Tuesday. Press 3 if you are willing to press a few more buttons before we help you." Didn't you feel special?

Or the time you called the airline to change a reservation only to hear a tinny voice say, "Thank you for calling White Knuckle Airline. Your call is very important to us. Please stay on the line for the next available agent. Your estimated wait time is more than 10 minutes." How important did you feel?

Or the time you called your doctor when your do-it-yourself project went awry and you were left with blood oozing from your right arm. Remember? You got a recorded message directing you to "Press 5 to connect to the nurses' hotline." As you attempted to apply a one-handed tourniquet to the source of your bleeding, the hotline message asked you to "Type in the first four letters of the last name of the person you wish to speak to." Seriously, do you know the last name of your doctor's nurse?

Or the time you took an important client to lunch at a restaurant that had come highly recommended. The waiter made a mess of your orders, dribbled coffee on your client's sleeve, and assured you, with a saccharine smile, that "a 21-percent gratuity has already been added to your bill for your convenience."

Now, if I were to ask your clients to describe three examples of exceptional customer service that they have enjoyed in your firm in the last couple of months, what would they answer? Or, would they have a story similar to the ones above?

Identifying client expectations.

When a client hires you, that person comes armed with certain expectations. The client may have been mind-tripping all the way to your office about how to spend the generous sum the court will surely award for his injury. That's one common set of expectations.

Another client may feel that her claim of construction defects in her new condo is actually quite minor, and that it will be quickly resolved if you'll just write a brief letter to the builder threatening a lawsuit. That's another set of expectations.

Let's consider yet another set of expectations law firm clients harbor that has to do with how you and your staff will treat them. Understanding these expectations is the first step in making your clients happy.

It's pretty simple, really. Think about the last time you took your car in for repair. You probably expected what most of us would expect:

- an accurate estimate of the cost of the work;
- the final cost would not exceed the estimate;
- the work would be completed on time;
- the work would be done properly;
- you would be treated fairly; and
- the problem would be resolved.

When clients come to your office, their expectations are not unlike the expectations you had of your repair shop. Your clients expect to be treated fairly, to get a reasonably accurate estimate of the total cost of the work, to have the work done properly and on time, within the estimated costs, and they expect the problem to be resolved.

It stands to reason, then, that if you meet your clients' expectations, you'll have a bunch of happy campers spreading the good word about your services, right?

According to research the Xerox Corporation conducted, there is a strong correlation between the level of customer satisfaction *intensity* and the probability that customers will repurchase the firm's services and/or recommend the firm to their friends and family. Specifically, a summary of this research shows:

SATISFACTION INTENSITY INDEX	REPURCHASE RATE	RECOMMEND RATE
Performance exceeded my expectations	90%	96%
Performance has fully met my expectations	56%	71%
Performance has mostly met my expectations	12%	19%
Performance has only somewhat met my expectations	3%	3%
Performance has fallen short of my expectations	0%	0%

It is clear from this research that fully meeting your client's expectations isn't good enough. ***For optimum rehire and referral opportunities, you need to exceed your clients' expectations.*** In other words, you need to "WOW" them! Huh? "How in the world can I do that?" you are probably muttering right about now.

How to exceed your clients' expectations.

Simple. The way to exceed your clients' expectations is by meeting their needs, and you do that through value-added services.

Think back to your trip to the car repair shop. We've already examined some of your expectations; however, beyond your expectations, you may also have had a wish list of needs that you were hoping against hope someone would meet.

When I take my car in for servicing, my list of needs is frequently longer than my list of expectations. As an example, if I must leave my car for the day, I need a ride back home or to the office. Then, I need a ride back to the shop at the end of the day. Or I need a loaner car—free of charge would be lovely. Sometimes, it's not possible for me to get back to the shop by the end of the regular workday, so I need to be able to pick up my car after 6:00 p.m. If I have to wait while the car is being repaired, I need a clean place to sit (my definition of "clean" in an auto repair shop is a place where I can sit while wearing white!).

I'd like magazines that don't have black greasy fingerprints on the cover. A cup of coffee, made that day, would be very welcomed. And, so on. You get the idea. These are needs that have nothing to do with the work being done properly on my car. Rather, these are niceties that add value for me personally to the overall service I am receiving.

Value-added services meet your client's needs.

How do you know what will add value for your clients? The first step is to ask them. "What can we do to make this experience easier or better for you?" Then, ask again. Keep asking throughout your representation.

The answers may surprise you. Remember, they are individual to the client, so listen carefully. As an example:

- Appointments after normal business hours and/or on Saturday.
- A place to park the kids while the parent meets with the attorney.
- Smoke-free clothing on the attorney (potential for severe allergic reaction in clients).
- Billing twice monthly so the client receives more manageable bills.
- Phone calls only during client's lunch breaks on a new job.

There are attorneys who have already learned this lesson and they are meeting their clients' needs in big ways and small ways, but all exceptional ways, including:

- Paying for a rental wheelchair so a cash-strapped client can get to court.
- Giving out personal cell phone numbers.
- Offering a ride home from jail.
- Meeting in the client's office, home, or hospital room.
- Personally delivering papers to the client for signature.
- Returning all calls within 15 minutes (and, no, I am not making that up!).
- Sending the attorney's receptionist and secretary to cover the phones at the client's office so all employees could attend a coworker's funeral.

These attorneys exceeded their clients' expectations by identifying some of their needs and meeting them. You've got to believe that their clients feel pretty special with this kind of treatment. These practitioners understand how to "WOW" clients.

Your clients will have their own unique list of needs. Ask, ask, ask. Ask for the client's sake. Ask for your own sake. Ask your staff what your clients need (they hear it all).

- What value-added services would your clients appreciate?
- What value-added services do you offer?
- What additional services can you offer?
- How would this work?
- What must you do to provide these value-added services?
- Who will be responsible for these services (by name/title per service)?
- What value-added services can you provide that your competition doesn't?

Take a moment and consider your current level of customer service. On a scale of 1 to 10 (10 being "superduper, couldn't get any better"), how would you rate your firm? Yourself? More importantly, how would your clients rate you?

Now, let's get back to "need." Your clients share certain common needs, and they aren't all that hard to figure out. We all (your clients included) need to be recognized as individuals, to feel important (that we matter), to be kept in the loop, to be treated with honesty, respect and dignity, to be remembered.

I once asked a legal secretary friend of mine how she was able to deal with her boss's criminal defense clients (pedophiles, murderers, rapists, and so on). She looked a little surprised, and then said, "They are our clients. They deserve to be treated with respect. I always refer to them as 'Mr.' or 'Ms.' I say 'please' and 'thank you.' I serve them just as I would serve a guest in my home. I don't care what they are accused of. That's not important to me because it's not going to change how I treat them. It is my job, though; to make sure they have a superior experience with our office. That involves shaking hands, serving coffee, smiling, and being truly interested in their well-being. I treat them the same way as another secretary might treat her firm's corporate clients."

She's absolutely right. The firm's clients deserve superior care—regardless of their circumstances.

Give equal treatment to all clients.

Pro bono and low bono clients deserve to be treated the same as those who've put down large advance fee deposits or who pay their bills timely each month.

A few years ago, I was working with Darryl, attorney/owner of a three-attorney criminal defense firm that had a small branch office in a neighboring community. The caseload in that remote office was 100 percent court-appointed work, while the clients in his primary office were private-pay cases.

During the course of my research into the workings of Darryl's firm, I was intrigued by the uneven treatment of the two offices. The remote office matters were not added to the main office calendar. Cases from the branch office were not discussed in the weekly status meeting. Calls from the remote clients were returned within days, rather than the 1-2 hour turnaround for clients of the primary office. There was even a difference in attorney time spent on the court-appointed cases vs. the private-pay cases. Unlike the private-pay clients, the court-appointed clients did not receive a file folder to hold their copies of documents, on the occasions when the attorneys remembered to send them.

Darryl is a delightful fellow, one of the kindest, most caring attorneys I've ever met. That's why the differences in the treatment of the clients from the two offices were so hard to reconcile. When I mentioned my observations to him, he was truly stunned. He had been totally oblivious to the fact that in his firm all clients are not treated equally. Darryl was ashamed that he had somehow set the example for this inequity and that his associates and staff were following his lead. No one in the firm was overly concerned with clients' expectations from the branch office, nor did they seem to give much thought to any of their needs.

Even small gestures can "WOW."

A personal injury attorney once told me an almost unbelievable story about one of his recent clients. Seems the young man was severely injured in a horrible car accident. While he was expected to survive his injuries, the doctors were forecasting a hospital stay of many months. His family began the search for a good personal injury attorney to handle their son's case. When they finally landed in this attorney's office, they explained the circumstances surrounding the accident and the details of the injuries sustained by their son. They asked the attorney if he thought he could help their boy. He replied, "I'd like to meet your son personally. If you will give me the name of the hospital, I'll get out there this afternoon to speak with him."

The attorney was surprised to see that the parents had teared up as he spoke; but he was stunned when he learned the reason for the tears. The parents told him that they had spoken with three other attorneys in the area before coming to this office. Each of the other three lawyers had asked the parents to bring the young man to the office for a consultation. When the parents reiterated their son's inability to leave the hospital any time soon, each attorney declined to make a hospital call to meet the young man. The attorneys' disappointing responses probably provided a "WOW" moment to the parents – but, it wasn't a good "WOW."

Needless to say, Attorney No. 4, who was willing to go to the hospital to meet with the accident victim, got the case. In this situation, the client's need may actually have been greater than his expectations; thank goodness, he found an attorney who understood that.

I would offer **one caution**. When you want to "WOW" your clients, be careful not to let your value-added services become a detriment. As an example, I took my car for an oil change late on a December afternoon. We were enjoying a short breather between snowstorms, and I took advantage of the day by trying to do all of my year-end chores in one afternoon. Seems I wasn't the only one with that thought. The dealership lobby was full, and I ended up sitting outside on a chilly bench with temperatures in the low 30s.

I kept jumping up to check on the progress with my car (and to keep warm), and was thrilled when I saw that it had been moved from the pit area to the parking strip behind the garage. I gathered up my things and went in to the service desk, waiting for the call. And waiting. And waiting. Periodically, I went to look for my car. There it was, sitting all alone in back of the building. I finally asked about the delay and was told, "We're waiting for it to come back from the car wash." (If you've ever lived in snow country, you know there is no point in washing your car until snow season is over. The car will be a mess by the time you get home from the car wash.) I waited an additional 35 minutes for my car to go through the car wash, a value-added service offered by my dealership. Oddly enough, the free car wash, meant as a bonus, actually made me say "#$*%&#" rather than "WOW" that day. I didn't want to be pampered, I just wanted to finish up my errands and get home before the snow started again.

What is a value-added service for one client may not be for another.

Keep raising your own bar.

Now, I mentioned that you should keep asking what you can do for your clients throughout the entire attorney-client relationship; but ask one more time what you could do to make things even better for your client.

An exit interview is a great time to get yet more input on what you can do to meet your client's needs in the future. At the conclusion of your representation, sit down with your client for a debriefing. After talking about the client's case and the subsequent outcome, turn the conversation to your services and your client's satisfaction. The conversation might go something like this:

"We've been through a lot together over the past few months. I just want you to know what a pleasure it has been to work with you. Through it all, you have maintained your focus and your positive attitude. Your cooperation and responsiveness made my job all the easier. Here at the Redenbaugh Law Firm, we work hard to provide the best service to our clients, and I just want to make sure we're doing that. Please tell me what the best part was about working with our firm."

Listen carefully and take notes. Then, follow up with, "In an effort to continually improve our service, I'd like to ask your further help. What could we do next time that would make your experience with us even more satisfying?"

Not only are you getting valuable feedback on your customer service, but you are also sending your clients out the door thinking about what a terrific experience they had with you. [NOTE: While your client is thinking of you in such a positive way, be sure to ask for referrals before she leaves, and make sure she knows your firm's other practice areas, as well.]

If you've missed the opportunity to conduct an exit interview, the next best thing is a client satisfaction survey. Mail this out immediately upon the completion of your representation. Include a self-addressed, stamped envelope for your client's convenience; then, send a follow-up note thanking him for his response.

Your clients deserve your best service. Make sure they get it.

> *Tip: Exceed your clients' expectations by meeting their needs!*

10

FEE-SETTING METHODOLOGIES:
LESSONS IN HOW NOT TO SET YOUR BILLING RATES

For many attorneys, setting their legal fees is an imprecise, uncertain, and, at times, downright terrifying exercise. Get it wrong and you could restrict your lifestyle, find yourself working long hours trying to make ends meet, or even kill your firm.

Over the past 20+ years, I've asked hundreds of solo and small firm practitioners how they set their rates. Not surprisingly, there is a certain sameness to their responses:

- I look at what my competition is charging and then [charge the same/go $5 higher/go a little lower].
- I charge what the market will bear.
- I charge what I feel I'm worth.
- I go with a fee that sounds reasonable.
- I charge what I want to make per hour.

One attorney said, "Every couple of years, I just pull a figure out of the air, say it out loud, and if it sounds okay, I go with it."

The most interesting explanation came from Maggie, who said:

"When I left my former firm and went out on my own, I hadn't given any thought at all as to my fees. During my first initial consultation, the potential client asked me what I charge. I was caught off guard and couldn't think for a minute. Then, I remembered that I had written a check for $273 that morning to cover the month's parking fees downstairs. So, that's the figure I blurted out. I thought, 'If he hires me for even one hour, at least I've got my parking covered.' He didn't seem to think it was out of line, so I've just stuck with it. I have no idea if that's where I should be or not."

Let's take a closer look at some of the common fee-setting methodologies in use.

I look at what the competition is charging.

Would you ever let your competition set your rates for you? That would be crazy, wouldn't it? Yet, that might be exactly what you are doing. Think about it. How did you determine what you would charge for your services? As a starting point, you probably looked at what your competition is charging.

My first question would be: how do you determine who your competition is? Is Attorney X your competition because you have the same practice area? Years of experience? Geographic location? Value-added services? Accessibility? Track record? Practice size?

For the sake of argument, let's say that you and Attorney X both have family law practices. You have 15 years' experience and he has 22 years' experience. You both practice in the same part of town. While you have handled several high-profile divorces for the local gentry, you and X have both built your practices around handling divorces for the middle-class masses. You graduated in the top 5 percent of your class at Georgetown, while Attorney X worked his way through night school at a small unaccredited law school in Southern California. Should you charge the same rate or should one of you be charging more? If so, who would that be?

Don't look at me, I don't know. Are these factors even considerations in setting your rates? Maybe, but it really all begins with what it costs you to provide your legal services, and your personal financial needs. It's good to know what your competition is charging when developing your own pricing strategy and positioning yourself in the market; however, don't adopt another practitioner's fees simply to avoid the appearance of being overpriced. If you lockstep your billing rates with your competition, you're making the assumption that Attorney X's rate will cover your overhead and your desired compensation.

Let's take a closer look. Attorney X shares a small office suite with his law partner. When they formed the partnership, they made the choice to have no staff, go paperless, and share overhead expenses equally (about $3,500 per month for each).

Now, compare X's practice to your own. What are your monthly expenses? Higher or lower than X's? And, you still don't know what his compensation is.

The other unknown quantity here is X's billable hours. Part of the reason Attorney X and his partner chose a barebones business model is because they want to have more time for leisure activities. With a low breakeven point, they don't need to generate as much money as they did at their former law firm. On the other hand, if your overhead and compensation is higher than X's, you either have to work more hours or charge more than X just to break even.

So, if you let your competition set your rates, I say, "Give it up"—it's apples and oranges. While it's good to know what others are charging, your first consideration in setting your rates is *your* desired compensation and *your* overhead. Besides, if Attorney X is looking at his competition when setting his rates, he's probably basing his fees on what you're charging!

I charge what the market will bear.

Interesting. How did you test the market? Which segment of the market? At what point did you encounter price resistance? How much price resistance? What did your clients say about your new rates? How much business did you lose when you bumped your rates up?

While you certainly don't want to price yourself out of business, rare is the attorney who has actually tested the market when it comes to fees. When an attorney tells me that she charges, "What the market will bear," I always ask how she tested it. I'm usually met with blank stares. It seems to me most practitioners figure that what everyone else is charging is what the market will bear, and that by pricing themselves in mid-range, they will enjoy a nice, safe, client-attracting spot. I call this the "Goldilocks Syndrome." If you recall, Goldilocks didn't like Papa Bear's porridge because it was "too hot." She didn't like Mama Bear's porridge because it was "too cold." The little, yellow-tressed housebreaker liked Baby Bear's porridge best (and scarfed it all down) because it was not too hot, not too cold, it was "just right." Same with the ursine furniture. Mom's and Pop's chairs and beds didn't suit, but Baby Bear's chair and bed were "just right." Charging in the middle means you aren't too high or too low; you are "just right." Right?

In his best-selling book *Selling the Invisible*, Harry Beckwith warns about mid-range pricing:

> "Companies in many services essentially set their rates by studying the going, high and low rates, and then deciding where they fall in the quality spectrum. This unfortunate practice tells their customers exactly how good the company *really* thinks it is.
>
> . . .
>
> "If you are the high-priced provider, most people assume you offer the best quality—a desirable position. If you are the low-cost provider, most people assume you deliver an acceptable product at the lowest cost—also a desirable position. But if you price in the middle, what you are saying—again, is: 'We're not the best, and neither is our price, but both our service and price are pretty good.' Not a very compelling message."

What does your price say about you? The only way to truly test the market is to put your rate out there and see what happens. Remember, you aren't raising your rates just to be raising rates. Your rate is based on your overhead, your personal financial requirements, the complexity of the issues involved, your years of experience, the length of time in which you have to work, and so forth. Try your new rate for a month or two and see what happens. If no one hires you, then perhaps your rate is too high. Or perhaps you aren't doing a good enough job of selling yourself and your services. Or you haven't helped your potential client differentiate between your skills and services and those of the lower-priced attorney down the street. Or you haven't added sufficient value to your services to make you worth the higher price. Do you see what I'm getting at? Make yourself worth your new billing rate.

So, you try out your new rate and your potential client doesn't hire you. "That darned higher fee just cost me a client," you moan. Unless your potential client told you your fees are too high, you are merely assuming you weren't hired because you are charging too much. In some instances, that may be true; however, clients aren't as money-driven as attorneys would make them out to be. Case in point: Two criminal defense attorneys practice in the same community. One charges $165 per hour and the other charges $750 per hour. Oddly enough, the higher-priced attorney has turn-away business, while the lower-priced attorney (who is outstanding and has great experience) must rely on a court contract to help him supplement his private-pay fees and meet his financial needs each month.

You need to disavow yourself of the belief that money is always the deciding factor for clients when hiring an attorney. Sometimes it is, but most of the time, it isn't. While others may argue with me on this, I believe that clients are smarter than that. Price is not so important if the attorney is likable, exhibits integrity, promotes trust and confidence, is attentive to the client, and a personal connection forms.

Lou was an estate planning/probate attorney who hadn't raised his rates in a number of years. Long before I met him, I knew of Lou's reputation as an attorney of high integrity and superior legal skills. With more than 25 years' experience in drafting wills and trusts, Lou's skills level was outstanding, and he was a great and generous resource for less-experienced attorneys. I was surprised to find that Lou's fees were considerably below what other practitioners in the area were charging for estate planning services. [I know what you're thinking: "You just said you can't base your fees on what the competition is charging." Correct, but, I also said that it's good to know what others are charging in positioning yourself in the market.]

Lou and I spent quite some time discussing the fees for his various services, and the time involved in preparing the work product. Under his existing fee structure, the client would pay a flat fee for the basic will, and then could pick and choose which, if any, additional documents (durable power of attorney, health care directive, etc.) he or she wanted. All fees for subsequent documents were charged separately.

"Don't each of your clients need to have a health care directive, and durable power of attorney, for starters?" I asked.

"Yes, of course," Lou replied.

I asked why he gave them the option of not having these necessary documents. It seemed to me that if he was allowing his clients to leave his office without all of the documents they needed to have in place to protect themselves, their assets, and their heirs, then he wasn't providing complete service to them.

He admitted that some clients treated his fee schedule like a restaurant menu, looking at the far right-hand column to check the price before asking for anything beyond the basic will. I suggested that Lou have one all-inclusive price for an estate plan. In this way, the clients would be fully protected and the temptation to omit certain vital documents to avoid an additional fee was removed. I further suggested that he bump his rates up from $1,500 to $2,500 for an all-inclusive estate plan, based on his overhead expenses and the work involved in preparing the plan. [NOTE: Lou's typical client had assets ranging from $1-$7 million, so the value of his work to his clients was significant.] We also developed some additional services that other attorneys were not offering to add value to his package.

Terror overtook Lou and he just couldn't bring himself to raise his rates. Over the course of a couple of months, we revisited this issue several times, but he wouldn't budge. He was gripped with a common fear amongst attorneys, "If I raise my rates, I'll lose all my clients and never get another one."

[Does this ring a bell with you? Have you ever raised your rates? And you never got another client, right? That's what I thought.]

One day my phone rang and it was Lou. I could hear the smile in his voice when he said, "You'll be happy to know that I just tested my gag reflex."

I knew immediately that he had quoted his new higher rate. "So, what happened?" I asked.

"She whipped out her checkbook so fast that I never even got the sentence all the way out."

All that angst, all that fear—and for naught. Lou was surprised to discover that his market would bear more than he was charging. His signing rate was always good, but now it's nearly 100 percent. He believes that he's finally charging what his target market expects to pay—and can afford to pay—for a first-rate, all-inclusive estate plan. Lou's fee is now more commensurate with the value of his work to his clients.

I charge what I feel I'm worth.

This is a tricky way to set your fees because you are assuming that your clients share your opinion of your worth. My experience has been that most small firm attorneys undervalue themselves; so, it's just possible that your clients think more highly of your work than you do. If you charge what *you* feel you're worth, you may be undercharging.

For argument's sake, let's say you test your rates on the market and the market says, "You aren't worth it." You've got two choices: (1) pull back on your price, or (2) make yourself worth it. What makes you different from other law firms? What do you offer that no one else is offering? What can you do better than your competition? Why is your customer service superior to that of other attorneys?

If you need to increase your rates, but your clients aren't going for it, you've got to show them why you are worth more money, and you'd better make it good! Talk about your years of experience, show them the technology you employ in your work, speak of your dedication to seeing the job done right, describe your value-added services; in other words, sell yourself. Help your clients make their decision by showing them why you are the best choice for the job and your price will be less important.

I go with a fee that sounds reasonable.

Reasonable to whom? You are playing a fool's game if you believe that you know what your potential clients are thinking. When you discuss your fees during your initial consultation, don't assume the surprised look on your client's face means your price is too high. When a terrific DUI attorney quoted his fee to a potential client, the practitioner mistook the man's shocked look for price resistance. When the potential client stood up to leave without hiring the attorney, the practitioner believed his suspicions had just been confirmed, and silently cursed himself for his recent fee increase.

At the door, the client turned back and said, "I'm surprised by your fee. I've seen two other attorneys and they both quoted triple what you are charging. I figure I need the best attorney I can get, and at your price, you just must not be as good as them."

The attorney learned a lesson that day about what sounds reasonable. He thought his low rates made him look like a real bargain; trouble is the client thought he looked second-rate.

So, back to the question, "To whom does the fee sound reasonable?" [NOTE: You know by now that the answer better not be you!] What you cannot guess is the value of your services to the client. What fee would sound reasonable if you were able to keep a commercial truck driver from losing his driver's license after a DUI arrest? What fee would sound reasonable to the parents of a 15-year-old-child who was charged with selling drugs to classmates? What fee would sound reasonable to a brand-new homeowner whose condo developer refuses to do anything about a mold problem so severe that the owner had to move out?

While ethics rules require reasonableness of fees, there is no template by which to measure your rates. Remember the two criminal defense attorneys mentioned earlier—one charging $165 per hour and the other $750 per hour? Is $750 reasonable? It's hard to say until you can determine what the attorney brings to the table and the value of his services to his clients. While it is hard to imagine, $165 may not be reasonable for the other attorney's services. All you have to do is look in the back of your state bar magazine to read about attorneys who are unworthy of any hourly rate.

The key here is *sounds* reasonable versus *is* reasonable. The attorneys who set their rates in this manner are often truly saying the figure out loud to see how it sounds. (Remember the gag reflex?)

That's a scary way to set your fees. Your ears and your clients' ears may hear entirely different things in your rates.

Some guidelines for determining reasonableness include:

- complexity of the issues and work involved in the case;
- the attorney's experience with similar cases;
- the going rate in the geographic area;
- time and labor required;
- the likelihood that this work will preclude the attorney from handling other work (from other parties to this matter now or in the future, from other existing clients, from other potential clients, etc.);
- the dollar amount involved and the potential outcome for the client;
- the length of time and the circumstances under which you must perform your work;
- whether the fee is fixed, hourly paid, or contingent;
- the reputation, skills and ability of the attorney handling the case; and
- the terms of the written fee agreement and whether or not the client had received a full explanation of the agreement, the scope of the work to be performed, the financial obligation of the client to the attorney, the attorney's billing practices, and so on.

Sounding reasonable isn't good enough. Make sure your rate *is* reasonable.

I charge what I want to make per hour.

Great! How do you figure whether or not you are actually doing that? Do you start with what you want to take home, and then factor in write-offs and write-downs, your collection rate, your overhead expenses, etc? If so, go for it. If not, please know that while your desired compensation should definitely be a consideration in setting your fees, you can't look at this number alone to determine what you will charge.

In looking at some of the ways in which attorneys come up with their fees, you have to wonder how so many of them stay in business? If you identify with any of these methodologies, do not despair. The next chapter reveals a simple formula to help you determine what your minimum hourly rate must be to cover your overhead and give you the personal income that you want. Read on!

> *Tip: In setting your fees, if your methodology doesn't make sense, you may only make cents!*

11

YOU ARE NOT YOUR COMPETITION:
GETTING YOUR BILLING RATES RIGHT

Okay, we've had our fun poking holes in some of the more common rate-setting methodologies; but you still need to figure out what you should charge. The good news is that there really is an easy and precise way to calculate your minimum hourly rate, and you'll feel a lot more secure when you know that your rate is correct for your needs. We're looking at the minimum hourly rate because several of the popular billing methods are based in whole or in part on the expectation of earning a certain amount of money per hour.

Let's help Charlene figure out her minimum hourly rate. A solo family law practitioner in a traditional brick-and-mortar office, Charlene has one full-time legal assistant. So as not to price herself out of the market, Charlene chose to adopt the billing rate being charged by several other family law attorneys in her community. Even though she puts in long hours, and captures all of her time, there just never seems to be enough money.

The first thing I would tell Charlene is that she must take into account her overhead expenses, compensation, benefits, write-offs, write-downs, discounts, uncollectable accounts receivable, and expected firm profit when calculating her hourly rate. By merely following someone else's lead, Charlene is missing this critical point. It's no wonder it's not working for her.

By using a simple formula, Charlene can determine the minimum she needs to be charging per hour to cover her expenses and her compensation.

Charlene's Minimum Hourly Rate

Charlene's desired compensation	$	100,000
The firm's total overhead expenses (exclusive of Charlene's compensation)	$	164,100
Emergency fund (6 months x $22,008/mo. overhead & compensation)	$	132,050
Desired firm profit	$	25,000
TOTAL REQUIRED REVENUES	$	421,150

Charlene's realization rate (% of fees billed that she collected)

[Divide total gross fees collected by total fees billed]

Charlene's gross fees collected	$	287,500
Total hours billed		1,325
Charlene's current hourly rate	$	250
Total fees billed	$	331,250
Charlene's realization rate		
$ 287,500 ÷ $331,250 =		0.87
Charlene's projected billable hours goal		1,300
Total required revenues	$	421,150

Required Revenues ÷ (Realization Rate x Billables Goal) = Minimum Hourly Rate

or

$ 421,150 ÷ (0.87 x 1,300 hours = 1,131) = $ 373

Charlene is now faced with a dilemma. She is currently charging $250 per hour, but according to this calculation, she needs to bring in $373 per hour to cover her compensation, overhead, emergency savings fund, and desired firm profit.

For her geographic location, $373 is considerably more than any other family law attorney is charging. Unless she can prove that she's worth the extra money, Charlene's rate may put her out of reach for a good portion of her target market. Is there a solution for Charlene?

First, Charlene needs to review the figures she used to arrive at the $373 rate, starting with her desired compensation. Charlene wants to have a personal income of $100,000 per year. Is that realistic? Maybe, maybe not. We'll let Charlene hang on to that thought for now.

Next, Charlene should give her expenses a good going over. Charlene pays her assistant $45,000 per year and provides her with a small benefits package, including health insurance, Sep-IRA, two weeks' paid vacation, and an annual Christmas bonus. Aside from that, Charlene's monthly expenses run around $8,800 for office space, equipment, insurance, on-line research, supplies, dues, publications, and so forth. If her expenses seem to be in order, Charlene must then look at her realization rate.

At 87 percent, Charlene's realization rate is a little low. She's left about $44,000 sitting on the table in uncollected fees. While that isn't an extraordinarily high sum, it still has a significant impact on her small practice. If Charlene can boost her collections and get her realization rate up to 95 percent, she could bring her minimum hourly rate down to $341, still a lot higher than her current rate, and possibly too high for her target market.

So, let's go back to the component parts of her required revenues. If Charlene dropped her desired compensation by $10,000/yr and raised her realization rate to 95 percent, her required revenues would drop to $411,150 and her rate would be $333/hr. Then, if Charlene built her emergency fund up over, say, two years, instead of one, her required revenues would go to $345,125 and her hourly rate would be $280.

At this point, Charlene has several options to hit her required revenues. She can:

- Adopt the $373/hour rate and hope for the best
- Bill more hours at her current rate
- Find ways to decrease her overhead expenses
- Improve her collections, and/or take a larger advance fee deposit or use an evergreen deposit account to raise her realization rate
- Reduce her compensation
- Make herself worth this higher rate through value-added services, increased efficiency with technology or leveraging, or enhanced legal skills
- Adopt a hybrid billing method to deemphasize her hourly rate (e.g., hourly billing for certain tasks and fixed fees for others).

If you were in Charlene's shoes, which option would you choose?

Figuring the rates of others.

Now, let's say that Charlene has several other timekeepers working for her. How would she calculate their minimum hourly rates? For starters, Charlene is no longer 100 percent responsible for the firm's overhead; all firm timekeepers will share in covering the overhead. To figure the share for each, Charlene would turn to a simple weighting system. In other words, each timekeeper carries his or her weight (share of overhead) based on positioning in the firm. It would look like this:

Senior partner/owner	1.75 share
Midlevel partner	1.50 share
Junior partner	1.25 share
Senior associate (3+ yrs' experience)	1.00 share
Junior associate (less than 3 yrs' experience)	0.75 share
Paralegal	0.50 share
Legal assistant	0.25 share

Total all the shares and divide this number into the firm's overhead (exclusive of attorney compensation). The resulting figure is the value of a 1.00 share. Then, multiple this number by each timekeeper's weight to determine the dollar share of firm overhead. This is the number you will use as the overhead figure when calculating each timekeeper's hourly rate.

As an example, let's say there are four timekeepers in the firm: the owner, a senior associate, a paralegal, and the legal assistant. The total of their weights is 3.50. Overhead is $194,000 (without attorney compensation).

$$\$ 194{,}000 \div 3.50 = \$ 55{,}429$$

Multiplying $55,429 by each timekeeper's weight will give us the following:

Senior partner/owner	$ 97,000
Senior associate	$ 55,429
Paralegal	$ 27,715
Legal assistant	$ 13,857
TOTAL OVERHEAD SHARES	$194,001

Flat fees can make or break you.

Now, let's get back to Charlene's situation. If she decides to go with a flat (or fixed) fee for part or all of her work, she must be certain that rate is working for her. Charlene is basing her flat fee on the time she believes she actually spends on certain routine tasks or matters. I don't have a problem with Charlene using flat fees, but she has to prove to me that she's actually getting paid what she thinks she's getting paid for this work. The only way to know for certain is for Charlene to track all of the time she works on her flat fee tasks and cases. It's risky to guesstimate the time required to do anything, even routine tasks. The human tendency is always to underestimate and that can make a big difference in your bottom line, as evidenced by the case of Ryan and Steve.

Attorneys Ryan and Steve were offering simple wills for $75. They called this their *loss leader service*. Their strategy was to offer wills for a very low price to attract new clients who might be interested in their other services (at a higher fee, of course). If nothing else, they hoped to handle the probates of these wills at some point in the future. Sounds like a plan, doesn't it?

It was obvious to me that a $75 will was more than a loss leader, it was a bottom line disaster. These two fine practitioners did not fully understand the impact of a $75-will on their revenues.

"A simple will takes no time at all to prepare. Probably no more than 45 minutes to an hour of our time," offered Ryan, in defense of their strategy.

To help them understand what their $75 fee was doing for them (or to them), I asked them to walk me through the will preparation process in their office.

"I'm a new client and I want a will. Tell me how this all works. What happens when I phone the firm for the first time?" I inquired.

"Our estate planning paralegal will ask you some basic questions, explain our fee, and then set up an appointment for you to come in to meet with me," Ryan answered.

"What happens in that first meeting and how long do you meet with me?"

Ryan replied, "Well, I would meet with you and ask you a number of questions to make sure I'm clear on your wishes and that I have a complete inventory of your assets. I'll also tell you about various other documents you might wish to have, such as the health care directive, durable power of attorney and so forth. This meeting would last about one-and-a-half hours."

"Great! Then what do you do after I leave and how long does it take?" I asked.

"I review all of my notes and fill in anything that I've missed. I then give my notes to the paralegal and she inputs this information into our templates. She returns the drafts of any documents to me for review. All of this takes only about 15-20 minutes of my time, and maybe 30 minutes of paralegal time." Ryan offered.

"Then what?"

"I review the drafts of all the documents, make any necessary corrections, and give it back to the paralegal. She inputs the corrections, prints out the documents, and prepares a cover letter asking you to review the drafts and return them with your comments by a certain date. That takes maybe another 30 minutes of my time and probably 15-20 minutes of paralegal time," Ryan replied, getting into the swing of things.

"And then?" I pushed.

"Once you've reviewed the will and returned it, the paralegal finalizes the document, incorporating your changes, and returns it to me for one last review. When I'm satisfied with it, she will call you to set up an appointment to come in and sign. This is probably about another 20-25 minutes for each of us."

"When I come in to sign, do I meet with you? Tell me what happens at this point," I queried.

"You do meet with me because I want to make sure that we've accurately captured your wishes and that you completely understand and agree with each document. I'll answer any last questions you may have and send you on your way, once you've signed the will. This meeting usually lasts about 30-45 minutes."

"Gotcha," I said. "So, based on what you've just outlined for me, you are spending upwards of three hours on a simple will and accompanying documents. Does that sound about right?"

"Yeah. Like I said, it's not much time at all," Ryan replied.

Ryan is right, it's not much time at all; however, the value of that time is far greater than the $75 he was charging. Based on his regular hourly rate, the value of this time was $525 or more.

The only way to know if three hours was anywhere near accurate would have been for Ryan and his staff to record all time spent on simple wills. While we didn't have that information available to us at the time, it was clear to Ryan and Steve that their strategy had a flaw.

They were shocked to see the difference between their $75 price and the $525 estimate that more closely reflected the value of the time involved in handling this work.

I asked the obvious: "You are currently losing $450 or more on each will. How's that working for you? How do you make any money at all on this?"

Quick-thinking Steve blurted out, "Volume!"

Lest you think I've forgotten about the cross-selling aspect of this loss leader strategy, let me assure you that I did not. Their other practice area? They had a contract to handle all of the court-appointed criminal defense work for the county. And the probates? They admitted that they had never handled a single probate of a will prepared by the firm. One of the primary reasons probably had to do with the fact that their small community is a Navy town. The folks looking for a quick, cheap will were mostly Navy personnel who were about to be deployed. Most of these clients were reassigned after a couple of years—off to live out their lives in parts unknown where other attorneys would handle the probates.

No matter how you looked at it, their loss-leader strategy didn't make sense. They were grossly underpaid for their work, they were apparently not developing long-term relationships with their clients, and they were not getting the second-tier work from their clients' estate plans that had been their primary goal in setting such low fees.

When you set your flat fees, it is important that you constantly monitor those fees for appropriateness. The only way to do that is **to *track all of your time every time*** on your flat fee work. There's a good chance your hourly rate isn't what you think it is for some of this work. When you've completed a flat fee case, divide the hours worked into the fee received and see what you earned per hour. Surprised?

Oh, Ryan and Steve? Never did another will, simple or otherwise. I certainly didn't have a problem with them doing estate planning; however, if they wanted it to be cost-effective (and why wouldn't they?), they needed to either:

- raise their rate to cover the actual time involved;
- make the process faster and more efficient so it takes less time; or
- offer more service, not less, so that their clients would think that a newer, higher rate is still a good value.

Don't fear a rate increase.

If getting your billing rate right results in a need to increase your fees, the chart on the following page should help allay some of your fears about losing clients. As an example, if your gross margin is about 50 percent and you raise your rates by 10 percent, you can lose up to 16.67 percent of your clients without dropping a penny in income. You can, and should, expect some loss of clients with a rate increase, but one way to ameliorate the potential for loss is to keep current clients at their present rates for a period of time, and quote your new higher rate only to new clients. If you decide to raise your rates for existing clients too, then consider carefully how you will do that. One gentle way is to give a decent amount of advanced warning in a letter.

It may sound counterintuitive, but you want to have about a 10-15 percent price resistance factor. That's the percentage of people that psychologists tell us will complain about everything, regardless. If someone complains about your rates, figure they belong in this 10-15 percent group. If everyone complains, rethink your fees.

Your rates shouldn't fit everyone, but they should fit your ideal client. You need to understand your target market—what they can afford to pay, and what they expect to pay, for legal services. If your target market can't afford what you need to charge, then you've either got to bring your fees in line with their ability to pay, or you need to rethink your target market. Investing in new technology to increase your efficiency and productivity, leveraging your practice with lower-paid associates or paralegals handling much of the work, using contract attorneys, going virtual, or getting better at collecting what you're owed are a few of the strategies that will help keep your fees at a level that is acceptable to your clients.

Sample Language for a Fee-Increase Letter

Dear _____.

I want to tell you just how much we have enjoyed working with you over the last _____ (months/years). I particularly enjoy our conversations and you have made my job so much easier with your (fill in the blank with some admirable quality/trait) _____ [e.g., quick responses to my requests, ability to understand the issues quickly, ability to stay focused, immense patience with the slow pace of the legal process, etc.].

As with so many other businesses across the country, our firm has experienced a significant increase in operating expenses this past year. After much consideration, we find that we must increase our hourly fees as follows:

Harvey Siders, partner	$ 275
David Guinn, associate	$ 225
Sherrie Barker, paralegal	$ 100

We value your business and look forward to continuing our work together in the future. To honor our relationship, we will continue to bill all work on your matter at your current rate until _____ [a date 60-90 days in the future], at which point we will move to the new fees. All new clients and new work will be billed at our new rates effective immediately.

Thank you for your continued business. It is our great privilege to serve you. Our relationship with you is very important and we hope that you feel the same.

> **Tip:** *If you aren't making enough money, first look at how you set your billing rate.*

CALCULATE YOUR MINIMUM HOURLY RATE

Revenues for Which You Are Responsible

Your desired compensation	$	_____
Your share of the firm's total overhead expenses (exclusive of attorney compensation)	$	_____
Emergency fund	$	_____
Desired firm profit	$	_____
TOTAL REQUIRED REVENUES	$	_____

Your Realization Rate (% of fees billed that you collected)

[Divide total gross fees collected by total fees billed]

Your gross fees collected	$	_____
Total hours billed		_____
Your current hourly rate	$	_____
Total fees billed	$	_____
Your realization rate		

$_____ ÷ $_____ =   _____

Number of hours you expect to bill this year   _____

Total required revenues $ _____

Required Revenues ÷ (Realization Rate x Billables Goal) =
Minimum Hourly Rate

or

$ _____ ÷ (_____ x _____ hours = _____) = $ _____

YOUR EMPLOYEE WEIGHTS

POSITION	WEIGHT	DOLLAR VALUE
Senior partner/owner	1.75	
Midlevel partner	1.50	
Junior partner	1.25	
Senior associate	1.00	
Junior associate	0.75	
Paralegal	0.50	
Legal assistant	0.25	

THE IMPACT OF A FEE INCREASE

RATE INCREASE

(% drop in revenues you can sustain to maintain your same
gross profit after a rate increase)

GROSS MARGIN

AMOUNT OF INCREASE	35%	40%	45%	50%	55%	60%
5%	12.50%	11.11%	10.00%	9.09%	8.33%	7.69%
10%	22.22%	20.00%	18.18%	16.67%	15.38%	14.29%
15%	30.00%	27.27%	25.00%	23.08%	21.43%	20.00%
20%	36.36.%	33.33%	30.77%	28.57%	26.67%	25.00%

12
ALTERNATIVE BILLING METHODS:
ONE SIZE DOESN'T FIT ALL

After relying on hourly, fixed, and contingent fees for many years, attorneys are getting more innovative in their billing methods in an effort to meet the needs of their clients. If you have been locked into traditional billing for some years, perhaps there is an alternative billing method that would actually be better suited to your practice and your clients. Let's look at some of the ways attorneys are currently billing for their services.

- *Hourly rate* – probably the most widely used billing method, and still in use by many small firm practitioners. This form of billing requires contemporaneous timekeeping on a task-by-task basis throughout the day. With hourly billing, the client bears the risk by not knowing what the end cost will be.

- *Contingent fee* – as defined in a written fee agreement, the attorney receives a preset percentage of any monetary award or settlement the client receives. The important question here is whether the percentage is calculated on the gross recovery, or on the net amount remaining after expenses are deducted. The risk is borne by the attorney here because she receives no money if she doesn't win the case or obtain a settlement for her client.

- *Hybrid contingent fee* – the attorney takes a smaller percentage of the monetary award or settlement, and in exchange, the client pays the attorney a reduced hourly rate or a lower flat fee. This reduces the risk for the attorney associated with handling contingent cases, and can result in a higher payout to the client from the final award.

- *Fixed (or flat) fee* – the attorney charges a predetermined fee based on the expected time required to handle certain fairly routine matters, such as estate planning, DUI defense, uncontested divorce, and so on. The attorney bears risk here because unforeseen events or issues may materialize that will require more attorney time than originally estimated. On the other hand, the client knows exactly what his financial obligation will be for the services to be provided.

- *Value pricing* – the attorney and the client agree on the value of the attorney's services in procuring certain results for the client (usually spoken of in terms of savings to the client). As an example, the attorney may receive 25 percent of the first $200,000 in savings to the client, and 30 percent of any savings realized above $200,000. This may be a one-time payout, or may continue on for several years. In other words, the savings may not be immediate, so the attorney receives a percentage of cumulative savings over a period of time. The client has an expectation to a certain extent of what he will pay the attorney, and the attorney receives payment based on the value the client receives from the attorney's services.

- *Unit pricing* – either a fixed amount of time or money is charged for the different tasks or phases of representation. As an example, the attorney may always charge 0.2 hours to read and respond to e-mails or for phone calls, and 2.5 hours for drafting a motion, regardless of the time actually involved. (If a phone call only takes four minutes, the client is still charged 0.2 hours. If the call takes 20 minutes, the client is charged only 0.2 hours.) Depositions may always be billed at a flat rate of $2,000 per day, and trials at, say, $75,000, again regardless of the actual time involved.

Attorneys are beginning to see that billing can be accomplished in a variety of ways. I've been hearing for years that hourly billing is now passé, but I sure haven't seen a rush to embrace alternative billing methods in small firms. It seems to me that hourly billing provides a certain amount of comfort to the attorney because he knows that he is getting paid for the all of the time he puts in on behalf of his clients. The clients, on the other hand, may believe that hourly billing allows attorneys to pad their bills or drag out the work to get more money. Finding a billing compromise that satisfies both the client and the attorney's needs would seem to be a worthwhile goal.

I don't believe it's necessary to give up hourly billing entirely, but I do like the idea of hybrid fees: combining two or more billing methods to fit the client and the case. The hybrid contingent fee was mentioned above, but let's consider other combinations, as well, starting with an hourly rate combined with unit pricing. With this hybrid fee, the attorney charges an hourly fee for the time actually worked on what I would term open-ended tasks (e.g., answering interrogatories, on-line research, or other tasks for which the attorney's time cannot be estimated in advance with any real accuracy), and a fixed amount of time for routine tasks (e.g., phone calls, e-mails, etc.). I think the reason some attorneys don't charge for these little bits of time is because they see them as just little bits of time. Nevertheless, these snippets add up over the course of a year. By using unit pricing (really, just mini-fixed fees), you can insure that you are more nearly paid for all of the time you work for a client.

The best part is that you don't need to record your time; just indicate a phone call or an e-mail on your timesheet and you're done.

A DUI attorney switched to a hybrid fee when yet another client hit him with a surprise after he had begun representation. He quoted a fee of $5,000 to handle the DUI; the client agreed and paid him the money. After the attorney got a copy of the police report, he discovered that his client was also charged with an injury hit-and-run, but had failed to mention that to the attorney. When he called the client, the client said, "I just figured that's all part of the fee because I was charged at the same time I got the DUI."

The attorney learned several lessons here: his fee agreement wasn't sufficient because it didn't detail (or limit) the scope of the work to be undertaken, he didn't ask enough questions in the initial consultation, and clients sometimes either knowingly withhold information, or don't tell the attorney everything because they don't think it's important.

This practitioner has since revised his fee agreement to specify the limits of the work he will perform for the fee. In addition, he has added in a clause that allows for hourly billing if other unforeseen circumstances arise, and then goes on to list some of the things that might cause him to bill beyond the fixed fee. He was really glad he did, because this exact same scenario occurred a couple of years later – only this time he was covered and got paid for the extra time spent on the hit-and-run charge.

A law firm in Seattle has chosen an interesting variation on value pricing. They keep time records and send monthly bills to their clients, just as they've always done; however, several years ago, they initiated a new practice. On the bottom of their monthly bills is a statement that reads something like this:

"Please feel free to adjust the amount you pay up or down, depending on the value you feel you received from our services."

Risky? You bet. But according to one of the firm's attorneys, they are doing just fine, thank you very much. They do good work, build strong relationships with their clients, and provide exceptional customer service. It's not unheard of for their clients to pay *more* than the amount of the bill because the clients' perception of the value received from the firm's services often exceeds the fees charged.

A young solo practitioner uses only value pricing for his services. Unfortunately, he sets the amount with the client *after* the work is done — and, we all know how quickly the wild enthusiasm for your skills and expertise dies off once a case is over. He admits that sometimes he comes out okay, and sometimes he takes "a real bath" (in his words). The trick to value pricing is to determine the value of the various possible outcomes *before* you do the work.

If you think maybe it's time for you to revisit how you charge for your services, do a little research before you make your decision. Which billing methods would work best for your practice area and your clients? Better yet, how would your clients like you to bill for your legal services? Talk to your best clients about the type of billing method you might develop to serve their needs and still get you paid. How can you get paid for the *value* of your services to your clients (something hourly billing doesn't allow for)?

The legal industry has been around for centuries, but hourly billing is only about 50 years old. Just because it has some history now doesn't mean you have to hang on to it. Think how a change in your billing method might better serve your practice and make your clients even happier, at the same time.

What could work for your practice?

> ***Tip:*** **Break from tradition and find the most advantageous way to bill—for you and your clients!**

13

ADVANCE FEE DEPOSITS:
PAYMENT INSURANCE

At the outset of the attorney-client relationship, several things happen that provide you some assurance of the client's commitment to the work and the relationship. One such occurrence is the client's execution of your written fee agreement. Another is the client's payment of an advance fee deposit against a portion of your projected fees and costs.

Asking clients for money can be difficult; however, your fee agreement can both open the door for a discussion of your fees, and do the asking for you. A detailed written fee agreement lays out your policy on advance fee deposits, and the amount of money required before you will begin work on the client's matter.

In accepting an advance fee deposit, you are making a promise to your client that you will act as the client's attorney, that you will protect the client's best interests, and that you will perform the required legal services timely, and to the best of your ability. Your client has made a commitment to you by providing the deposit, and you have made a commitment to the client by accepting it.

Attorneys frequently use the terms "advance fee deposit" and "retainer" interchangeably. This is not correct, as they do not serve the same purpose, nor are they handled in the same manner vis-à-vis the attorney's trust account. [NOTE: Check your local ethics rules for guidance on the use of advance fee deposits, flat fees, and retainers.] A retainer secures an attorney's promise to be available to the client at some future point. The attorney does not bill against a retainer because it is not meant to cover fees and costs. An advance fee deposit is exactly that, a deposit against future fees and costs that will be incurred on the client's behalf. The attorney bills against the advance fee deposit and pays the billed fees and costs from the client's trust account until the deposit is consumed.

The concept of an advance fee deposit is relatively new. When I began working in the legal industry more than 30 years ago, I never heard the term "advance fee deposit." While larger corporate clients often supplied a retainer, most representation began with a handshake between attorney and client. From there, the attorney simply billed for services as they were rendered. Nowadays, it is standard practice to take some money up front to cement the relationship and protect the attorney.

Getting money up front helps you get paid.

When a small firm is having cash flow issues, the trouble sometimes stems from the attorney's policy on advance fee deposits. Either the firm does not require an advance fee deposit, or the amount requested is not sufficient to protect the firm from a no-pay or slow-pay client. Unless you take your entire fee up front, or are handling contingent cases, it's just good business practice to ask for an advance fee deposit for each new matter. The deposit serves several purposes. It:

- helps to insure timely payment to the attorney;
- demonstrates the client's commitment to see the case through; and
- provides a good start to the attorney-client relationship.

A successful advance fee deposit policy requires:

- asking for sufficient money up front;
- clearly explaining your advance fee deposit policy in your written fee agreement; and
- obtaining the client's signature indicating understanding and acceptance of your policy.

Asking for a deposit equal to at least the first two months' worth of billings in each new matter works for many smaller cases. If you were involved in a high ticket matter, then you would require an advance fee deposit that is more in line with your total projected legal fees for the case. As an example, you might require anywhere from 20-50 percent, or more, of projected fees up front.

To better understand the need for the advance fee deposit, let's consider the case of Attorney Tom and his client David. Now, David and his wife Pinky are not getting along, and on March 26, Pinky serves David with divorce papers. On April 2, David hires Tom to represent him in his divorce. As part of their agreement, David gives Tom an advance fee deposit of $1,000.

The first few weeks on any new case can be quite time-intensive for the attorney, especially in family law. Lots of papers to be filed, research to be done, letters to be sent, documents to be reviewed, and so forth. David's case is no different. Tom does a lot of work in the first four weeks of representation. On May 1, Tom sends David a bill for $2,100. Per Tom's written fee agreement, if payment of the statement is not received within 10 business days, Tom will apply the amount in David's trust account to his bill. David does not pay within 10 days, so Tom removes the $1,000 from the trust account as partial payment for his bill.

Tom is busy practicing law (and working on David's matter), so he isn't paying close attention to David's account. In fact, Tom doesn't realize that David didn't pay the May 1 statement until June 1, when he is again preparing his client bills. At this point, David owes Tom another $2,250 – on top of the $1,100 remaining unpaid from the prior month. Tom's June 1 statement indicates a past-due balance as a reminder to David that he hasn't paid the prior month's bill. And, Tom continues working on David's matter until July 1, when he prepares another bill with an even larger past-due balance. The chronology of David's account looks like this:

April 2	Advance fee deposit received	$ 1,000
May 1	Tom sends statement for April work	$ 2,100
May 12	Tom applies money from trust account to David's bill	- $ 1,000
May 12	Balance in trust account	-0-
May 12	Balance remaining unpaid on statement	$ 1,100
June 1	Tom sends statement for May work ($2,250) and the past-due balance ($1,100)	$ 3,350
July 1	Tom sends David a bill for his June work ($2,325) and the past-due balance ($3,350)	$ 5,675
	TOTAL BILLED FOR 3 MONTHS	$ 6,675
	TOTAL RECEIVED	$ 1,000
	TOTAL UNPAID BALANCE	$ 5,675

From this example, it's easy to see how accounts can quickly become seriously past due. Had Tom asked for a $5,000 deposit (his projected fees for the first two months), the April and May statements would have been paid in full, along with a portion of the June bill. The potential loss to the firm from David's unpaid fees would have been significantly lessened.

With a traditional advance fee deposit policy, Tom would place David's deposit into the client trust account, and withdraw monies as earned. Tom wouldn't have the chance to learn that David is a no-pay client until the deposit is totally exhausted, and Tom might be unable to withdraw at that point. So, Tom would be forced to continue working without getting paid.

Tom has handled many divorces over the years, and he has learned important lessons. First, he knows how much work is typically required in the first couple of months of a divorce proceeding. Second, Tom has discovered that family law is one of the hardest practice areas in which to get paid timely and in full. Indeed, it is not uncommon for a family law attorney to receive partial payments throughout representation; then receive the remaining monies owed from the proceeds of the sale of the family home after the divorce has finalized.

Evergreen deposits keep cash flow evergreen.

For better protection, Tom would like to minimize the financial downside of a family law practice. He can do this by requiring an advance fee deposit, with a twist.

Handled properly, the variation on a traditional advance fee deposit, known as an *evergreen* or *replenishing* account, can make all the difference in the world in your cash flow. With an evergreen deposit account, you put the advance fee deposit into the trust account, send out your monthly bill, and pay that bill out of the trust account if payment is not received within a certain period of time. [NOTE: Check your local ethics rules for the minimum number of days you must allow for payment of your bill before withdrawing funds from your trust account.]

An evergreen deposit differs from a traditional advance fee deposit in that your client is still responsible for paying your monthly bill, even though you may already have paid yourself out of the trust account if payment was not received timely. If the client's check arrives before you withdraw trust account funds, you treat it as a regular payment on account and deposit it into the firm's operating account. If the client's check arrives after you have already paid yourself from the trust account, deposit the check into the trust account to return the client's deposit balance to its original level. Your client must understand and agree to the terms of this advance fee deposit as set forth in your written fee agreement.

Your billing statement should display a notation alerting your client to your policy of withdrawing the amount due from the trust account if the client does not dispute or pay the bill within a certain number of days. As an example, that notice might look something like this:

"You have [10] days from the date of this statement to either dispute the fees and costs herein, or remit payment in full. If we do not receive payment from you and you do not dispute this statement, we will assume that you approve these fees and costs and will withdraw the money to pay the balance due from your client trust account."

If the client neither disputes nor pays your bill, you pay yourself from the client's trust account. If there isn't enough money in the client's trust account to satisfy your bill, then the client is responsible for paying any additional amount due, in addition to restoring the trust account to its original level.

If the balance in the client's trust account falls below a predetermined amount (as stated in your written fee agreement), you will stop work, as allowed, until the client restores the trust account to its original level. If the client is unable, or refuses, to replenish the deposit to its original level, you need to be prepared to file a Notice of Intent to Withdraw, as allowed.

While I believe that the practice of law is a business, it should be a business with a heart. On a case-by-case basis, you may wish to negotiate some other arrangement regarding unpaid bills and the required trust account balance for a good client who is going through a rough spot. For instance, you may agree to a lower trust account balance (e.g., $2,500 instead of $5,000), or you may allow the client extra time to replenish the account.

To see how this all works, let's look at how Attorney Arissa handles Client Whitney's advance fee deposit:

8/8	Whitney gives Arissa an advance fee deposit	$ 2,500
9/1	Arissa bills Whitney for services rendered	$ 1,750
9/15	Arissa withdraw funds from Whitney's trust account to pay the bill	- $ 1,750
9/15	Whitney's current trust account balance	$ 750
9/23	Arissa receives Whitney's check and puts it in the trust account	+ $ 1,750
9/23	Whitney's trust account balance is restored to its original level	$ 2,500

As you near the end of your representation, bill the client as usual, but indicate "DO NOT PAY" on the invoice to allow you to use up the remaining money in the trust account. When you have completed all work, the client is responsible for paying any additional sums owed you. On the other hand, if you have been paid in full, any outstanding balance in the trust account must be promptly returned to the client.

An evergreen deposit account:

- insures that you are paid regularly;
- allows you time to identify problem clients before their accounts become excessively past due; and
- gives your clients peace of mind in knowing that you have been paid, even if they are a little late in sending in their payments.

But, my client can't afford a deposit.

What's that you say? Your client can't afford a sizable advance fee deposit? Okay, how much can your firm afford to write off in unpaid fees and costs? When you don't require an advance fee deposit, you are putting your firm at risk of sustaining a loss. Look at it this way, if your client can't come up with a deposit now, how will he be able to pay your bill at the end of the month?

Call me crazy, but it seems to me that if the client can't come up with your advance fee deposit, he might not be able to afford your services at all. I may be a minority of one on this, but I don't believe you are acting in your client's best interests if you run up fees and costs that the client cannot afford. While you may resolve the client's legal issue, you are also saddling your client with a huge debt and adding to his stress level.

The bottom line is this: regardless of the type of advance fee deposit you choose to use, establish your policy and stick to it. Get sufficient money up front to protect you and your client, or refer the client to a lower-priced attorney or a legal services clinic for more affordable help.

> *Tip:* *Protect yourself from a write-off and your client from having you withdraw by requiring an advance fee deposit!*

The following is sample language covering the evergreen deposit account that can be incorporated into your fee agreement. [NOTE: Please check your state's ethics rules to insure you are in compliance before instituting this practice.]

EVERGREEN TRUST ACCOUNT

Sample Language for Including In Your Fee Agreement

Prior to commencement of representation, the Client will provide the Attorney with a deposit in the amount of $ _____. This sum will be deposited into the Attorney's trust account in the Client's name. On or around the _____ day of each month, the Attorney will provide the Client with a statement of all fees and costs incurred on the Client's behalf during that billing period, as well as the balance remaining in the Client's trust account. Full payment of the statement is due within [e.g., 10 days] of receipt. If full payment is not received within [10] days, Attorney will apply any funds in the Client's trust account to the outstanding balance due on the Attorney's most recent statement of fees and costs. If the Attorney's billed fees and costs exceed the balance in the trust account, Client is responsible for paying the additional amounts due, as well as the amount necessary to return the trust account to its original balance of $ _____.

If the balance in the Client's trust account drops below $ _____, all work may cease and the Attorney has the option of filing a Notice of Intent to Withdraw unless the Client provides the funds to return the trust account to its original level. At the conclusion of the matter, any remaining funds in the trust account will be applied to the Attorney's final statement, in which event Client will be responsible for any amount due over and above the remaining deposit balance, or the Client will be entitled to a refund of any amount remaining after the final statement is satisfied in full.

The Attorney reserves the right to bill the Client other than on a monthly basis, at the Attorney's discretion, should the case so require. The Attorney may also request additional fees from the Client at various times during the case, should the funds in the trust account be insufficient to cover services performed or anticipated services to be rendered. If the Client is unwilling or unable to comply, the Attorney may cease work on the case and withdraw. In such event, a Notice of Intent to Withdraw will be sent to the last known address of the Client.

14

THE GOOD, THE BAD AND THE UGLY:
INADVERTENT PRO BONO

Pro bono, arguably, one of the most beautiful phrases in the legal lexicon, refers to the noble act of providing legal services without charge to individuals and organizations of limited means. I think this is attorneys at their finest.

Inadvertent pro bono, on the other hand, isn't noble at all. This is what your legal services become when you don't get paid for all the work you've done, even though you fully expected to be paid. Indeed, this unpaid work does not constitute pro bono work at all. The only reason your services were free is because your client didn't pay you as agreed at the time of hire.

Seriously, is there an attorney anywhere who hasn't had to write off unpaid fees? I doubt it. Every attorney has horror stories about difficult clients and cases that went south on them. Frequently, these terrifying tales end with, "and then she refused to pay the rest of the money she owed me" or "he threatened me with a malpractice suit if I tried to collect the balance of my fees." With many attorneys, it's not a matter of whether they've ever been stiffed on a fee, but, rather, how much they had to write off. This situation is especially harmful to small practices, as they don't always have the financial resources to cover the loss.

To be fair, not all clients set out to rob their attorneys. Some were naïve about the total cost of their matter and are unable to pay the bill. Others lost their case and had to pay the other side, and there simply isn't enough money to go around. Some clients are forced into bankruptcy because of the cost or outcome of their case, and still others weren't happy with the outcome or their attorney, so they refuse to pay. Regardless of the reason, the effect is the same, you don't get paid what you are owed.

Poor management can create the problem.

While no-pay clients will always exist, there are times when attorneys must own some of the responsibility for this frustrating and painful situation. The breakdown of certain management functions only exacerbates this problem. Specifically, you increase the risk of not getting paid your full fee if you:

- fail to adhere to an Ideal Client Profile;
- fail to collect an adequate advance fee deposit;
- fail to collect all of the flat fee up front;
- fail to guide the client's expectations of fees and costs right from the beginning;
- don't use a written fee agreement;
- fail to accurately record all of the time you worked on a matter;
- exert a high level of pressure on attorneys to generate revenues "no matter what";
- fail to properly monitor aged accounts receivable (aged accounts report);
- fail to implement and enforce a standardized collections process for past-due accounts;
- fail to communicate regularly, timely, and clearly with the client;
- fail to bill regularly, timely, and accurately for all fees and costs;
- fail to withdraw when you see you aren't getting paid; and
- fear pursuing your client for past-due fees.

What's a poor lawyer to do?

If giving away unplanned free services is a problem for you, there is hope. The first step may be hard, but it's necessary. Stop taking anything and everything that walks through the door! The red flags are flying, alarm bells are ringing, and it just may be your imagination, but you could swear you see a faint image of a little red figure holding a tiny pitchfork over the potential client's left shoulder. Despite all this, you find yourself eagerly reaching for the client's check. You know what's going to happen when you go against your gut instincts. You've walked this path before, and it always ends up in the same place. Why would you possibly think this time will be different?

I can understand the fear associated with turning away work, especially when money is tight; however, *if the client can't afford you, or you sense that you will have problems getting paid, you need to turn the client away.* [NOTE: You know what FEAR is, don't you? False Evidence Appearing Real.] You are taking a case, against your better judgment, because you need the money; yet, the irony is that you probably won't get paid anyway, so what have you gained? The potential for a major headache – and a major write-off? Nancy Reagan was right, "Just say 'No.'"

Some attorneys seem to believe that there is a karmic quality to turning away a client. If they turn away a client—even a bad one—they will never get another one, they won't have any money, and they'll be driven out of business. Okay, maybe that's a bit of an exaggeration, but more than a few practitioners believe that they will be punished in some way for turning down work. Have you ever suffered some sort of divine punishment for turning down a client or case? How about your colleagues? It just doesn't work that way.

If you've ever provided unplanned unpaid legal services, take a minute to think back to that situation. Is there anything you could have done differently that would have resulted in a more positive outcome? How could you have protected yourself from this eventuality? What lessons are you taking away from this sad experience?

Pro bono work is a wonderful gift from attorneys to their communities, and it helps insure access to justice for everyone in this country. Using your skills and knowledge to help others without pay is both a duty and a privilege. It can be quite satisfying helping someone who can't afford to pay you; yet, when you expect to be paid for your work and aren't, feelings of anger, frustration, and violation can set in. Protect yourself by tightening up your management practices and getting better at case and client selection. Do meaningful pro bono work of your choice each year, and develop practices and policies to help you get paid for all other work.

> *Tip: Set your pro bono goals and give away the work you choose, then choose to get paid for all the rest.*

15

GETTING PAID WHAT YOU'RE OWED:
HOW YOU BILL AFFECTS WHEN YOU GET PAID

Unlike a fine cabernet sauvignon, your accounts receivable are at their best when less than 30 days old—and they definitely do not improve with age. Quite the opposite, in fact. The older you allow your accounts receivable to become, the more they cost you and the less likely your chance of 100 percent recovery. The trick is to keep from building up past-due accounts in the first place. Stay on top of your accounts receivable and keep that cash flow pouring into your bank account.

Sometimes what you don't do can make getting paid more difficult than what you do. If you have cash flow problems, look at yourself first. For instance, do you have accounts that have shown no payment activity for more than 90 days? 180 days? Do you wait until the end of the day to record your time? Do you bill less frequently than once a month? Do you just keep sending bills showing an increasing past-due balance in the hopes that your client will suddenly pay up? Then, what you're not doing—pursuing past-due accounts, recording time contemporaneously, billing regularly—has contributed to your cash flow problem, whether or not you realize it.

The good news is that with a few simple adjustments to your existing billing practices, you can get paid, even out your cash flow, recover out-of-pocket expenses, and improve communication with your clients.

The first step to getting paid is a written fee agreement.

Your fee agreement is the foundation of the attorney-client relationship. It lays out in black and white the scope of your representation, and details what and how you bill for fees and costs, the client's responsibility to pay your bill, and what will happen if the client doesn't pay. The fee agreement should explain your billing practices, including:

- how you will bill for your work (including your billing rate, as well as the rates of others who will be working on this matter);

- how you will bill for costs incurred on the client's behalf;

- the day of the month on which you prepare bills and the manner in which you will transmit the bill to your client (e-mail, mail, fax);

- when the client's payment is due;

- the amount of any advance fee deposit required;

- the disposition of the client's advance fee deposit (client trust account or general operating account);

- when and how you will withdraw money from the client trust account; and

- your policy on past-due accounts (charging interest, cessation of work, withdrawal from representation, collections agency, lawsuit, etc.).

Although it's difficult for some attorneys, you really must discuss money with your clients during the initial consultation. Clients must understand and agree to your fees and your billing practices before you begin work. If you jump the gun and start work before the client has signed your fee agreement, you run the risk of (1) a bar complaint; (2) damaging your relationship with that client; and/or (3) not getting paid. If it's uncomfortable for you to have the money chat with your clients, you aren't alone.

Solo practitioner Ellen becomes almost nauseous at the thought of talking with clients about money, so she doesn't. She does use a fee agreement, but leaves blanks where her hourly rate and advance fee deposit figures should be entered. As the clients leave her office, Ellen asks them to "stop by my assistant Mona's desk and hand this agreement to her." You can imagine her clients' surprise when Ellen's assistant fills in the blanks and asks for a $3,500 advance fee deposit! It's a really clumsy way to treat clients, and a poor start to the attorney-client relationship. You have to suspect that some of her clients are mad at her before they even leave the office.

To get paid what you're owed, record your time.

Capturing your time as you move through the day is the only way to know that you are being fair to your clients and fair to yourself with your billings. You don't want to overcharge your clients; on the other hand, you certainly don't want to perform work for which you aren't paid, unless it is planned pro bono work.

Here's what happens if you don't record your billable time contemporaneously. If you wait until the end of the day to record your time, you lose, on average, about 10-15 percent of your potential billable time simply because you cannot remember every single thing you did during the day, nor the time involved. If you wait until the next day, your average loss will be 25 percent or more of the time you could have billed. The end of the week? Fifty percent.

Let's take a look at what this can mean to your firm. Do you think, perhaps, it's possible that you fail to capture six minutes per day? It could be a quick phone call with a client, an answer to an e-mail, or a brief consultation with your paralegal on a client matter—six minutes that you don't record. If your hourly rate is $200, your billing rate is $3.33 per minute. Now, let's say that you lose six minutes each day. Here's what that looks like:

$$\begin{array}{rl} \$ & 3.33/\text{min} \\ \text{x} & \underline{\quad 6 \text{ mins/day}} \\ \$ & 19.98/\text{day} \end{array}$$

$$\begin{array}{rl} \$ & 19.98/\text{day} \\ \text{x} & \underline{\quad 5 \text{ days/wk}} \\ \$ & 99.90/\text{wk} \end{array}$$

$$\begin{array}{rl} \$ & 99.90/\text{wk} \\ \text{x} & \underline{\quad 48 \text{ wks}} \end{array}$$

$ 4,795.20 ANNUAL LOSS

If you think you may be losing 15 minutes, or 30 minutes, or more, do the math. There is no question that if you aren't recording your time contemporaneously, you are losing potentially billable time. How much can you afford to lose each day?

The other thing about failing to record time contemporaneously is that we always underestimate the time it took us to do something. Case in point is my client, Jean. Now, Jean was a good attorney, but she just couldn't seem to get her time down on paper even weekly. When the bank account got perilously low, she would close her office door and devote the day to trying to recreate her time for the past few weeks so that she could send out bills. Every time she went through this little exercise, Jean would promise herself that she would get better with her timekeeping. It never happened.

In desperation, she bought a popular timekeeping software program with the hope that it would provide an easy way for her to capture her time. Jean did find the program easy, but not in the way she had hoped. Somehow it was easy for Jean to accidentally delete the program from her hard drive (which she managed to do three times); however, she was never able to use it effectively to capture time.

One day, as she was ushering me into her office for our appointment, her secretary interrupted us with an important message for Jean. Her client Jennifer was calling from the East Coast. Jean turned to me and said, "I've really got to take this call. We've been playing phone tag for more than two weeks and I must speak with her."

I said, "Take your time," and retired to the lobby to wait. On the table next to my chair was an office phone, and I could see that Jean's extension light was shining brightly, and it continued to shine, and continued to shine, and continued to shine. Finally, Jean ended the call and came out to retrieve me.

When we got into her office, she started to ask about a particular issue we had been working on, but I interrupted saying, "Did you record the time for that phone call?"

"Oh, right," she said, fishing around for something to write on. "Let's see, the client was Jennifer, today's date is the 15th, and we talked about the proposed property settlement her husband submitted." She happily scribbled away.

"And how much time did you spend on the call?" I asked.

After staring at the ceiling for a moment, Jean wrote down, "20 minutes."

"That's great," I said. "Your billing rate is $300 per hour, so at the end of the month, you'll be able to bill $100 for this call. See how easy this is?"

"It is easy," Jean exclaimed. "I don't know why I have such trouble doing this."

"There's just one little problem," I said. "You were on the phone for 1 hour and 40 minutes."

"No way," Jean protested.

"What time was our appointment?" I asked.

"Two o'clock."

"What time is it now?"

"Quarter to four," she replied.

Jean had just written off $400. Accurate timekeeping requires you to note both your start and your stop times. Whether you use your computer or a yellow legal pad to record your time, the important thing is to get it all recorded correctly. You can't bill for time you didn't record. Don't leave money on the table—make sure you are capturing all the time you actually work.

I think the best way to develop your timekeeping discipline is to take my 30-day challenge. For 30 days, record all of your time every day, billable and nonbillable alike. Yes, it's a pain, but I think you'll find at the end of the month that you captured more time than usual. If it takes 21 days for us to form a new habit, then 30 days of recording all your time ought to make timekeeping such a routine part of your day that you won't even notice you're doing it.

Billing statements don't just present your fees.

As recently as the 1970s, firms would send out tersely worded billing statements on the first of each month, just like clockwork. The bills contained four words, "For Professional Services Rendered," followed by a dollar amount. Clients seemed to be okay with these statements because, for the most part, they paid the bills without complaint. Over time, however, clients have become less inclined to accept vague billing descriptions, and now expect a detailed accounting of the services provided (and, even then, they will sometimes still question the bill), before they'll write the check.

Unlike those simple billing statements, smart attorneys have learned that a properly constructed bill serves three purposes. Your billing statement is a tool to:

1. *Communicate with your client.*

   Your bill tells the client what you've been doing on her behalf during this billing period. It will help the client stay current on the case, even if you aren't a great communicator in other ways.

2. *Market your services to your client.*

   Your bill should clearly demonstrate the value of your services to your client. Clients are much more likely to pay a bill when they see that the various phone calls, research sessions, and conferences with opposing counsel have a direct benefit to them. (This is a great way to remind your client that you were the best choice for the job!)

3. *Collect money from your client.*

   Use it to collect money owed to you for legal services and out-of-pocket expenses.

If your bill isn't serving all three purposes, you're missing out. Maximize the value of your bill to your attorney-client relationship and you will be more likely to get paid without a fuss.

Let's take a closer look at what your bill is saying to your client. Does your bill look something like this?

7/6/09	Conf. w/opp couns	0.8 hrs
7/17/09	T/C /client	0.4 hrs
7/29/09	Research	3.3 hrs
	TOTAL HOURS BILLED	4.5 hrs
	TOTAL FEES DUE	$ 900.00

Now, tell the truth. Do you see a value of $900 in this bill? Would you even know for sure what your attorney had done for you from this bill?

Unfortunately, some attorneys turn out bills that look just like this. Some of the top time and billing software programs offer ridiculous looking formats that are more appropriate to a shipping bill than to a billing statement from a professional office. These programs also automatically use abbreviations, but you need to remember that your clients may not understand common legal abbreviations. What's an "opp couns," for Pete's sake? Or a "T/C/client?" "Research" on what, and why? What's in it for me, the client, and was it really necessary to spend 3.3 hours doing this?

Staying in your client's shoes for a moment longer, how about this instead:

7/6/09	Conference with opposing counsel Mr. Brown to discuss an equitable division of the household furnishings, division of the Royal Doulton character mug collection, and presentation of Mary's plan for a fair division of the children's school vacation and holiday time between herself and her husband	0.8 hrs
7/17/09	Telephone conference with Mary to discuss opposing counsel's counterproposal to the proposed property settlement and an alternative plan for the children's school holiday time	0.4 hrs
7/29/09	Conduct on-line research into past case law in support of Mary's claim for sole custody of the children, restrictions on foreign and interstate travel with the children, entitlement to the Royal Doulton collection, and spouse's responsibility for providing health insurance for Mary and her children	3.3 hrs
	TOTAL HOURS BILLED	4.5 hrs
	TOTAL FEES DUE	$ 900.00

While wordier, the more complete descriptions tell the client exactly what she is paying for, and the direct benefit to her of each action taken. The bill satisfies two criteria: (1) it communicates to the client what services the attorney performed during the billing period, and (2) it demonstrates the value of those services to the client in a manner that is easily understood.

Clients deserve bills that are both decent looking and understandable. If that requires typing out individual bills, then so be it. If you can achieve this with your software, better yet. Is it a lot of work to type out your bills? Sure. Is it too much to type them out for your clients' benefit? No. Remember what—and who—is most important here.

Bill promptly and regularly.

Many years ago, an attorney approached me following a CLE, stuck out her hand to me, and said, "Hi, I'm Elaine, and I haven't billed since February." Her words were startling in two ways: first, that's an odd way to introduce oneself, and second, it was a few days before Memorial Day weekend and February was but a distant memory.

As we shook hands, I asked, "Is that your goal—semiannual billing?"

"No, of course not," Elaine replied.

"What is your goal?" I inquired.

"Monthly billing."

"What's the block?" I pushed.

"Me. I'm the block. I hate doing the billing. I've got all the latest software, but I've never learned to use any of it because I hate the whole idea of billing so much."

On the rare occasion that Elaine did prepare bills, each statement had a "P.S." offering a 15 percent discount if the client would pay the bill in full within 15 days. No one ever took advantage of the offer, nor did they pay within 15 days, or 30 days, 45 days, or, in some cases, 60 days. In fact, her past-due accounts were astronomical.

Through further questioning, Elaine admitted that her clients frequently called to ask what they owed her. Many expressed frustration at the infrequent billings, and her cash flow was definitely all one way (out) due to her reluctance to tackle the chore. Elaine obviously had some problems around billing, so we agreed to meet the following week, after the Memorial Day weekend.

When I arrived at her office the following Tuesday, Elaine was grinning from ear to ear. She could hardly wait to tell me that she had spent 39 hours preparing bills over the long weekend. At her hourly rate of $200, her 39-hour marathon represented $7,800 worth of her time. What a shame she couldn't have put some of that time into billable work.

It was obvious to me that preparing bills was not the best use of Elaine's time, but she rejected my recommendation that she outsource her billing and bookkeeping tasks. "I don't want to lose control, and besides, no one will prepare my bills exactly the way I want them." I suggested that she have her legal assistant prepare bills under Elaine's supervision, but that wasn't an acceptable plan to her either.

She had three different billing programs on her computer, and had learned none of them. Elaine wanted a quick fix, but refused all of my advice, even when I showed her that spending her time on billable work, rather than on preparing her bills, could add another $1,500 or more to her revenues each month. At the time, she could have hired someone to handle her books and prepare her bills for about $300/month. That's a $1,200 net gain each month. Elaine would have none of it.

That was the first time I realized my limitations as a consultant. I learned that I can help clients set up systems and procedures to increase productivity, efficiency, and profitability— but I can't do anything about the gray matter between the ears. Elaine had her own agenda, and she was going to hold tight to that no matter what. Control was obviously more important to her than getting paid, treating her clients fairly, or living without constant worries about money. I have no hope to this day that her clients are receiving more than two or three bills per year, or that Elaine's cash flow has improved, or that her stress level around money has reduced at all.

Another attorney, George, had a similar problem. He managed to get the bills out every three or four months, but the infrequency didn't bother him all that much.

"My clients are just wonderful," George insisted. "They worry about me so much. Many of them call every month to see what they owe me. They're worried I'm not making enough money."

In Elaine's situation, I suspect she has some major issues around money because she is so afraid to deal with it. [See chapter 17 on "How Attorneys Underearn"]. In George's situation, he lived his life from one crisis to the next. His legal work was always done under the most extreme pressure, a messenger waiting in the lobby at 4:15 p.m. while the copier cranks out copies of a pleading to be filed that afternoon. Client bills were handled in much the same way. As an example, when George realized that quarterly taxes were due next week and he didn't have money to cover the bill, all other work stopped immediately, and the entire office went into billing mode. Because billing hadn't been done for a few months, preparing the bills was much more complicated than it should have been. Time records were misplaced, billing descriptions were incomplete, and write-offs were common. There's no way of knowing how much money he lost by delaying his billing, but I'm sure it was a considerable amount over the course of a year.

While it may seem like a no-brainer that bills need to go out at least once a month, it always surprises me to meet attorneys who don't bill with any regularity. In a large firm, it's perhaps not so noticeable when one attorney doesn't bill regularly because everyone else is billing and sufficient money is coming in to cover expenses. In a small firm, however, erratic billing causes all sorts of problems.

So far, we've only looked at sporadic billing from the attorney's point of view. Let's consider how your clients view the infrequent bill.

How inconsistent billing affects your clients.

Your clients are constantly watching you. They want reassurance that you care about them, that you are competent, that you are diligent in your representation of them, and that you are reliable. They check for indicators every chance they get. And, whether or not you realize it, you are constantly giving them input on all their concerns. If your fee agreement says that you bill on the 1st of the month, then you'd better get those bills out on the 1st. Your clients are watching.

Beyond that, your clients are just like you and me; they make budgets so they'll have sufficient money to cover their bills. And, like you and me, if an expense does not materialize as expected, we sometimes apply that allocated money elsewhere.

As an example, let's say that your client Sybil has budgeted $500 to cover your bill this month, but the bill never comes. So, Sybil tries her best to hang on to that $500 until she receives your bill. Next month, she anticipates your bill again, and puts aside an additional $500, but her car stalled on the way to work last week, and she had to dip into your money to cover the repairs. It wasn't much of a problem, though, because she still had no bill from you.

Now, Sybil's getting worried because she only has $700 of the money she thinks she probably owes you (but, doesn't know for sure) left in her account. After the third month with no bill, Sybil says, "Nuts to you." and goes off for a weekend retreat with her girlfriends to get rid of her stress (some of it due to the fact that she knows you're running up a big bill and she's wondering when it will hit and how she'll ever pay it).

When Sybil finally receives your bill for $2,000, with the notation on the bottom of the statement saying, "Payment is due within 10 days. Interest of 1 percent will be added to all past-due accounts," she is stunned, panicked, and angry. Sybil hasn't got a lot of money but she thinks you've got a lot of nerve, expecting her to pay four months' worth of legal fees within 10 days. She figures that because you weren't in a hurry to send the bill, she won't be in a hurry to pay. Because she doesn't pay quickly, you get tough with her and start your collections process.

I've seen this situation up close. Early in January one year, a friend of mine asked an attorney she had worked with some years earlier to help her set up a corporation for a new business she wanted to start. He was happy to help and took care of all the necessary filings, licensing, etc. Over the next 10 months, my friend would occasionally phone this attorney with a quick question. She was very grateful to him that he was apparently doing this work pro bono out of friendship, and with the idea that once her business took off, her need for legal services would grow and he would begin billing then. What a wonderful man he was!

In early December of that same year, when my friend received a bill for $7,350 for legal services for the past 11 months, she discovered that laziness was the cause of the attorney's lack of billing, not friendship and fond memories of days gone by. To make matters worse, his firm tacked on 10 months' worth of interest on her "past-due" account, along with a note that said, "Your account is seriously past due. If payment is not received within 10 days, your account will be sent to a collections agency." Nice guy, indeed.

George's clients weren't calling because they were worried he didn't have enough money. They were worried they were going to get hit with a huge bill, which eventually would have happened to them, as it did to my friend. Trust me, when it comes to paying attorneys' fees, clients are never worried that you aren't making enough money. They are worried about how much they will have to come up with once your bill arrives. It's simply not fair or respectful to your clients to hit them sporadically with super-sized bills because you don't get the bills out regularly.

Never forget that your billing statement is a communication tool, and it may not always communicate through the written word. Infrequent statements may be telling your clients that you are lackadaisical, disorganized, disinterested, or unreliable.

Improve your cash flow and keep your clients in the loop by billing promptly.

When you bill matters.

Now, let's consider your billing cycle. Do you bill at least once a month? (And don't even think about saying "No.") Do you sometimes feel anxious about money around the middle of the month? Do you have nightmares about not meeting payroll, losing your home, or having your power shut off?

In your spare time, try analyzing the payment patterns of your clients. Many law firms share a similar pattern of receipts. They receive a flurry of payments within the first 10 days after bills are mailed; then, payments slow up for another couple of weeks. Another flurry occurs in the five to seven days leading up to the next billing date because clients know that another bill is about to arrive and they don't want to pay an interest charge, nor do they want a dunning call from your office.

If you find uneven patterns in your cash receipts, consider splitting your client list and billing half on the 5th of the month, and the other half on the 20th.

"How will this help my cash flow?" you ask. Good question.

The following represents the cash receipts pattern that I've just described.

TYPICAL PAYMENT RECEIPT PATTERN FOR MONTHLY BILLING

BILLS MAILED	FLURRY OF PAYMENTS	SLOWDOWN	FLURRY OF PAYMENTS
1st of the month	3rd – 12th	13th – 23rd	24th – 30th

Whether or not this is the exact pattern of cash receipts in your firm, you probably have noticed a pattern of some sort. If that pattern has ups and downs, then billing half and half will help even out the peaks and valleys. A twice-monthly billing cycle would look like this:

PAYMENT RECEIPT PATTERN FOR TWICE MONTHLY BILLING

BILLS MAILED	FLURRY OF PAYMENTS	SLOWDOWN	FLURRY OF PAYMENTS
5th of the month	7th – 16th	17th – 27th	28th – 3rd
20th of the month	22nd – 1st	2nd – 12th	13th – 19th

Not only can you even out your cash flow, but also it should relieve those mid-month panic attacks when you envision facing your staff empty-handed on payday. I think one of the reasons some attorneys bill sporadically is because of the time involved in preparing and mailing the bills. The more you can break up the task, the less onerous it is, and the more likely you will be to actually get it done. One of my clients has gone where I dared not even hope—she just moved from monthly to a different form of twice-monthly billing. Each of her clients' receives a bill roughly every two weeks. While it is a little more work for her bookkeeper, her clients love getting smaller bills, they pay quickly, and her cash flow has improved dramatically.

Expense recovery made easy.

This last billing tip will help you recover direct out-of-pocket expenses incurred in-house. Specifically, we're talking about the expenses I call "The Four Ps:"

- Postage
- Phones
- Photocopies
- Phax (poetic license)

Some attorneys believe their fees adequately cover these costs, while others keep copious logs for every copy made or stamp used on behalf of a client. I don't support either of these strategies, and here's why.

The firms that consider certain direct expenses as being part of the regular cost of doing business have probably never done a cost analysis to determine how much they are absorbing each year for these out-of-pocket expenses.

The partners in a five-attorney firm claimed that these regular costs were "inconsequential" and had little impact on the overall profitability of their firm. When asked for a breakdown of expenses for these four services, the firm's bookkeeper and its CPA came up with what they termed "a very rough and definitely lowball estimate" of $25,000 annually. It didn't take the three partners long to realize that this admittedly lowball estimate meant $8,000+ out of each partner's pocket. They no longer considered these costs "inconsequential."

Logging these services requires way too much manpower, both in logging and in processing the charges for billing purposes, to make it worthwhile. Electronic tracking systems are a little better, but it still takes some effort on your part to make this feasible, and there's the cost of the equipment. So, what happens when you get to the copier and find you've forgotten to bring the client number for the tracking device? Do you just enter the admin number to save a trip back to your desk?

Besides, how can you possibly figure the actual out-of-pocket expense for a photocopy? How do you factor in the cost of staff or attorney time spent walking to/from and standing at the copier, plus the cost of paper, toner, electricity, equipment lease, per-square-foot rent for the floor space, etc?

If you bill out at $200 per hour, your rate per minute is $3.33. Do you add on attorney time for stuffing the envelope, walking to the postage meter, running the envelope through, and placing it in the outgoing mailbox? If that whole process took you six minutes, you'd have to charge upwards of $20.00 per postage stamp. Good luck explaining that to your clients!

Actual cost for long-distance phone calls would have to include, at a minimum, the federal and state taxes, connection fees, linebacker fees, etc., and possibly the value of the time spent reviewing the phone bill and allocating the calls by client. The point is this: no firm charges actual cost for these in-house services because no firm knows what that actual cost is.

There's a simple and pain-free way to recover direct expenses incurred in-house: charge a flat two or three percent of monthly fees to cover postage, photocopies, phones, and fax. For example, if you bill your client $100, you add an additional $2 or $3 to cover these costs. If you bill $1,000, you add $20 or $30 for costs. This is all clearly explained in your written fee agreement and your client agrees to this practice by signing the agreement.

Per your fee agreement, this cost recovery method does not preclude you from passing through actual costs incurred by sending large copying projects to your local copy shop, for instance. This plan also does not cover expert's fees, messenger fees, parking, mileage, special supplies, or any costs other than the four listed above.

Let's say that one month you were in depositions for your client for 10 days and you didn't have any need for photocopies, postage, faxes, or long-distance calls. You are certainly free to waive the flat fee for expenses that month if you choose.

Simple, easy, clean.

Past-due accounts need not be a fact of life.

Sometimes getting paid what you're owed involves collecting on past-due accounts. Okay, you've done everything right, everything you can to help yourself get paid for your work. Sometimes, however, despite your best efforts and sound practices, you may find yourself struggling with past-due accounts. As long as attorneys bill for their services, there will be past-due accounts. The key is to catch them early and keep them from becoming excessively past-due. Let's look at how two small firms handle their aged receivables.

Joe's four-attorney firm has a strict policy on past-due accounts – basically, they are unacceptable. The attorneys tell you that in the initial consultation, it says so in the written fee agreement, and the phone call you receive when your payment is late is yet another reminder that you agreed to pay timely, and the firm is holding you to that promise.

Joe's policy is simple – payment is due within 10 days of receipt of the statement. The firm allows one day for mail on either end, but if payment is not received by the 12th day, you get a phone call from the bookkeeper. It's a very pleasant call, but it's clear that they mean what they say in the fee agreement.

"We've noticed that we haven't received your payment yet this month. Is there something wrong? Can we help you in any way? Would it help you if we broke the amount due down into two payments, with the first payment due on Friday, and the second payment due the following Friday?"

The bookkeeper never hangs up without a firm commitment from the client to make payment, and the client's agreement that the bookkeeper may phone again if payment isn't received as promised. She always sets up a payment plan to insure full payment before the next bill goes out. On revenues of several million, the firm had only $12,000 in past-due accounts. Amazing!

Don's firm also works hard to avoid past-due accounts. The attorneys collect a deposit up front; however, it acts more like a security deposit than an advance fee deposit. It goes into the client trust account and just sits there. Clients have two weeks to pay their bills; if payment is not received within two weeks, the firm pays the bill out of the deposit, refunds any overage, and fires the client. This policy is explained clearly in the fee agreement, and the attorneys make sure the clients understand this practice during the initial consultation. Don swears he can count on one hand the number of clients the firm has fired via this policy in the last nine years. He also swears their receivables decreased significantly once they started taking a tough stand on payments. As he tells his client, "We aren't a bank. We are not in the business of carrying 'loans' for clients. Your credit card company demands timely payment or they cut off your credit. Your doctor demands timely payment or they won't treat you again. We're just doing what other businesses do." Do they ever bend the rules? Sure, but this is their stated policy.

Reduce those receivables.

To stay on top of your accounts receivable, review your cash flow report and your aged accounts report weekly. In looking at your aged accounts report, do you see accounts that are more than 180 days old? Unless those are contingent cases, or your client is on a payment plan, those old accounts will be hard to collect. The older you allow an account to become, the less chance you have of collecting 100 percent of the fees due. If you have accounts that haven't received a payment in more than a year, write them off. They are costing you to carry them on your books. If you want to take one last shot at collecting, be my guest; however, if that doesn't work, get rid of them.

With a small firm, I expect to see no more than about two months' worth of revenues in outstanding receivables. If you average about $23,000 in revenues each month, then your receivables shouldn't exceed $46,000. Carrying receivables means you are carrying risk. When your receivables become excessive (say, more than three months' of revenues), your risk moves into the really uncomfortable zone. If none of your past-due accounts paid another penny, would your firm survive? That's how you need to look at your receivables.

I learned long ago not to count my money until I see the green of the cash. Many firms could survive a loss, it's just a matter of how much of a loss.

Contrary to what many attorneys believe, having high receivables is less about the clients and more about the attorney's management skills. Specifically, getting paid involves the attorney's:

- case and client selection skills;
- ability to communicate billing procedures and expectations in both the written fee agreement and the initial consultation;
- requesting an adequate advance fee deposit;
- ability to capture all billable time;
- prompt and regular billing practices; and
- following up on past-due accounts early on.

If, despite all of your best efforts, you still wind up with a severely past-due account, you have some options available to you:

- take the client to lunch and take one more try at getting paid;
- turn the account over to a collections agency;
- enter into fee dispute arbitration;
- sue the client; or
- let it go.

Obviously fee dispute arbitration is only appropriate in certain situations. If you are just dealing with a deadbeat, then he's not going to go for arbitration. He just doesn't want to pay you under any circumstances.

If you choose to sue your client, only do so if you did your best work for the client, you kept great notes on your dealings with the client, your malpractice insurance is in place (and hasn't got a clause prohibiting you from suing a client), and you can withstand a possible countersuit. Consider whether you would be better off handling this matter in another way.

If you want to try to salvage the relationship, then making one more effort to get paid is the way to go. If you simply write it off, but continue to accept work from the client, you're the one with the problem. Case in point: Jack and his client, Luke.

In a meeting with Jack and his partner, I was reviewing their aged accounts report when I noticed one account that was showing $32,000 in the 180+ days column. I asked the status of the account, assuming the client was on a payment plan. Wrong.

Jack told me that it was "a really sad story." It seems that Luke and Jack were long-time friends. Sadly, Luke had experienced a string of bad luck, and that's why his account was in arrears. First, Luke was in a terrible car accident and his injuries prevented him from working for many months. Jack handled his case and got an $800,000 settlement for Luke. Even though Luke had signed Jack's fee agreement, Jack put his customary contingent fee "on hold" because "Luke needed all the money he could get right then." But, as Jack assured me, "Luke is good for it."

As his recovery progressed, Luke needed a steady income. Luckily, he found a business to buy with the rest of the settlement proceeds and, luckily, his friend Jack handled the transaction for him. Jack sent a bill, but Luke couldn't pay him right then because, as Jack said, "He needed to scrape together everything he could to buy his new business." But, Jack wasn't worried because, "Luke is good for it."

Then Luke's marriage broke up, Jack represented him in the proceedings, and Luke had to sell his business to pay off his ex-wife. Guess who handled the sale for $3.2 million. The wife got part of the money, and Luke kept the rest, – and, despite sending his bill, Jack got nothing. After all, "Luke needed every penny to help him get back on his feet." No worries. Jack knew that Luke would be paying him as soon as he could because, after all, "Luke is good for it."

Luke bought a second business; Jack again handled the deal and sent a bill, to no avail. Luke bought a luxury waterfront home, and Jack prepared all the paperwork. Then, Luke sold the second business and took an early retirement. Still no money for Jack, despite his regular bills, but Jack trusted his old friend because, "Luke is good for it."

I asked how long this had been going on. Jack's partner got busy looking at the carpet, while Jack inspected the ceiling hoping to find a satisfactory answer there, I think. Finally, he offered, "Uh, about 12 years. There's no question that he's good for it, but he's just had all this bad luck."

"Bad luck?" I exclaimed. "He got a big settlement for his accident, got out of a marriage, bought and sold two businesses for millions of dollars, and now lives in a waterfront mansion. He got 12 years of legal services for free. He's owed you $32,000 for 12 years, interest free. Forgive me, but I'm failing to see the 'bad luck' in there."

Look for Lukes in your own aged accounts report. Hopefully, you don't have accounts that are 12 years past due, but they don't have to be that old to be uncollectable. If you're still doing work for a client with a seriously past-due account, stop the work and send the client to collections, or write it off. I offer you words of advice on this issue: "If you're in a hole and you can't get out, quit digging!"

Put together your own collections policy and stick to it. It might look something like this:

1. A written fee agreement, signed by the client, which details your billing and collections practice.

2. Weekly aging of accounts receivable.

3. A personal phone call as soon as the account becomes past due.

4. A follow-up phone call within 24 hours if a promised payment is not received.

5. A firm letter stating your intention to stop work and file a Notice of Intent to Withdraw when the account is 45 days past due.

6. Cease work, as allowed.

7. Withdraw, as allowed.

8. Resolution through use of a collections agency, fee dispute arbitration, lawsuit, or write-off.

If you choose to use the services of a collections agency, do some checking on the company before you sign on. What is the fee? What age restrictions apply to past-due accounts (some won't take anything more than 90 days past-due)? How are calls handled? What is said? How tough does the language get? What tactics are used to try to recover owed monies? A good collections agency will let you call the shots. In other words, you can instruct them to stop short of filing a legal action against your client.

Pay attention to your aged accounts report. Be consistent in your follow-up. Respect yourself and your practice enough not to let clients take advantage of you. You worked for the money, unfortunately sometimes you have to do extra work to see that you get paid.

Never forget that you earned the money, and that you have financial obligations that you must meet. You've taken care of your client — now, take care of yourself and your family.

> *Tip: You are in business to provide legal services—not*
> *loans. Do everything you can to help yourself get paid!*

16

CHECKING YOUR FIRM'S VITAL SIGNS:
HOW TO MEASURE YOUR FINANCIAL HEALTH

Successful management of a law practice requires regular review of financial statements—both for what they say and what they don't say. Specifically, there are certain metrics by which to measure your firm's performance, but that information doesn't show up on a profit and loss statement, a cash flow report, or a balance sheet. Sometimes the most helpful information takes a little more digging. Luckily for you, someone else has already figured out how to do this in the simplest way possible. We're going to examine three of these metrics here: your turnover rate, liquidity ratios, and overhead-to-expenses percentage.

Let's start with your turnover rate.

How long does it take you to get paid for your services?

Unless you collect your entire fee up front, there's a good chance that you don't know how long it takes you to get paid, and the answer may surprise you.

XYZ Firm is a typical case. It is a second-generation law firm, founded by the father of the current managing partner. There are three partners, two associates, and two paralegals; seven timekeepers, in all. Most of the work is performed on an hourly basis, with a couple contingent fee cases and an occasional flat-fee estate plan thrown in for good measure.

When asked how long it takes them to get paid, the partners' answers were all over the board. Partner #1 said, "Our clients are pretty good, so I'd say 30 to 45 days."

"You're giving our clients too much credit. I think it's easily 65 to 75 days," proclaimed Partner #2.

Partner #3 said, "You are both off base. I betcha it takes 90 days or more for the money to come in."

It was clear they had never checked their turnover rate, the indicator of how many times they get paid in a year, and how long it takes to get paid.

While your turnover rate doesn't show up in your financial statements or your aged accounts report, it's not difficult to figure. In the case of XYZ Firm, the partners followed this simple equation to find their firm's turnover rate:

$$\frac{\text{Annual Revenues}}{\text{Accounts Receivable}} = \text{Turnover rate (number of times paid per year)}$$

$$\frac{365 \text{ days}}{\text{Turnover rate}} = \text{Number of days to get paid}$$

In football, a high turnover rate is disastrous; in business, it's the goal!

Remember the XYZ Firm partners' guesstimates? They were stunned to learn that it was taking them ***423 days*** to get paid!

Their very low turnover rate explained so much. The partners had not been able to take any money out of the business for five of the last 12 months. They had tapped into the firm's line of credit to cover payroll on several occasions. The tension between the partners was palpable, and the staff picked up on it. Everyone was holding their breath each payday to see if checks were actually being issued.

According to a survey conducted several years ago by Robert Morris Associates, the national average length of time to get paid for a law firm with less than $500,000 in assets is 11 days. How can that be? I doubt there is any one answer; rather, those firms may:

- collect 100 percent of fixed fees up front before the work commences;
- educate their clients as to the firm's expectations for prompt payment during the initial consultation and in the written fee agreement;
- bill promptly and regularly;
- establish a short due date for payments (e.g., 10 days from the date of the bill);
- tackle past-due accounts the day they become past due;
- take adequate advance fee deposits to insure they get paid;
- use an evergreen (or replenishing) deposit account so they are paid timely and in full every month;
- stop work or withdraw from representation (as allowed) for nonpayment; or

- selectively choose new clients, taking into account the client's ability to pay the attorney's fees, regardless of the outcome of the matter.

While you may never achieve the 11-day average, implementing strong billing practices and policies can help you increase your turnover rate and get you paid more quickly.

So, what's your turnover rate? You can't afford not to know.

Can you survive an emergency?

Now, let's move on to your liquidity ratios. For this, you'll need your current balance sheet. While your balance sheet isn't as fluid as your other financial statements, it's still an important management tool, and it provides information not available in the other reports.

Think of your firm's balance sheet as a snapshot of your firm at a particular moment in time. What's true of the firm today may not be true tomorrow. That said, the balance sheet reveals important information about your firm at the time the statement is prepared. The balance sheet shows your assets and liabilities, and owner's equity. It does not forecast earnings, showcase trends, reflect expenses, or give you a heads-up on your past-due accounts.

The balance sheet does, however, provide you with the numbers you need to calculate your firm's two liquidity ratios. The first, the quick ratio, is an indicator of how quickly the firm can raise money. This is definitely something you're going to want to know in times of crisis.

Your quick ratio is determined as follows:

$$\frac{\text{Most liquid assets}}{\text{Current liabilities}} = \text{Quick Ratio}$$

[NOTE: Your most liquid assets include cash, short-term investments, and accounts receivable.]

A ratio of 1:1 is acceptable; but 2:1 is better. If your liabilities are less than your current assets, then you have the ability to put your hands on money quickly in case of an emergency or an unexpected, large expenditure.

Part of protecting your firm and its employees is being able to get your hands on money quickly to meet unforeseen emergencies. Benny, an attorney in Olympia, Washington certainly suffered an unforeseen emergency when the 6.9 Nisqually Earthquake hit his area in 2000. The photographs told a startling tale: computers thrown across the room and smashed; pictures lying shattered across the furniture; files and supplies strewn knee-deep over every square inch of floor space. Insurance? You bet; but, despite what the TV commercials would have us believe, it took awhile to get the money from his claim. In the meantime, Benny had a law practice to run. He needed to relocate the firm, buy new equipment, notify his clients, continue to pay his staff until he had a place for them to work again, and take care of the damage suffered at home. He needed a lot of fast cash.

Harvey, a solo attorney in a small West Coast community, went into atrial fibrillation at 4:00 a.m. on a Tuesday morning. The doctors were unable to correct the rare heart problem they discovered, so he was referred to Mayo Clinic in Rochester, MN. Surgery was scheduled for the following week, and doctors warned Harvey that he would be off work for about six weeks. For a solo practice, that's hard news. His main worry was not his health. Harvey was worried that he would not be in the office to interview and take in any new clients who might be calling in his absence. Not only was he looking at an unexpected trip to the Midwest for he and his wife, but also major surgery, a lengthy recovery time, and no new clients for a six-week period. Harvey handles estate planning, so most of his clients come and go rather quickly. In his mind, coming back after surgery would be almost like starting over — a grim thought.

In both cases, these attorneys had some peace of mind because they had managed their firms carefully and each had been a good steward of their respective firm's money, and they had the quick ratios to prove it. Both knew where their money was, and that they could access it fairly easily. In each case, the attorney was able to weather the crisis and get back to work as soon as possible.

The second liquidity ratio, the current ratio, is an indicator of the firm's ability to meet its immediate financial needs (short-term obligations). [NOTE: Immediate needs include payroll, quarterly taxes, rent, insurance premiums, etc.] As an example, this might be a situation where you have a loan coming due. The current ratio is calculated as follows:

$$\frac{\text{Total current assets}}{\text{Current liabilities}} = \text{Current Ratio}$$

A ratio of 1:1 is acceptable. A ratio of 2:1 is considered strong. Again, your strength lies in having significantly more money available in assets than is tied up in liabilities.

While you may never need to test your firm's liquidity, it's still good to know your financial health; the quick and current ratios are just two more pieces in the overall picture.

Your overhead — what's too high?

How big is the bite your overhead takes out of your revenues? When attorneys tell me they aren't making enough money, the first place I look is at the firm's overhead. That's usually the first place the attorneys look, as well, but they don't always know what to look for. After reviewing their expenses, they jump to the conclusion that they have to cut overhead to make more money.

In a solo or small firm, I look for overhead to run 40-45 percent of revenues (exclusive of attorneys' compensation). I don't get worried until I see overhead at more than 50 percent of revenues. The highest I've ever seen was 97 percent. That means that 97 cents of every dollar that comes in goes toward overhead. That is not just a serious problem —that firm is on life support! Oddly enough, the attorney didn't see anything wrong with his overhead. Instead, he had self-diagnosed the problem as having more to do with the distribution of work amongst staff members. With advertising costs in excess of $240,000 per year for his solo practice, believe me, his financial situation had nothing to do with work distribution.

There is a sad story that tops that one, however. After one of my CLE presentations, an attorney, supporting himself on two canes, approached me and said, "I've got a new story for you to tell about overhead."

This gentleman had suffered a stroke the year before. He had been unable to return to work, but kept his office open in the hopes that his therapy sessions would one day allow him to resume his business. It was fairly obvious to me in speaking with him that his dream was not likely to happen. In the meantime, he had hired another attorney to handle all of his cases, and was giving the attorney all the money for the work he billed. He concluded his story by telling me that his overhead was running at about 135 percent of revenues.

So, you see, no matter where your overhead falls, there's probably somebody who is in much worse shape. That doesn't excuse your numbers, however, and you need to do some serious work if you're over 50 percent.

In 18 years as a consultant, I've found that, typically, the problem is not that overhead is too high—it's that income is too low. Sometimes the attorneys simply aren't billing enough time, or sometimes the realization rates are too low, indicating they aren't collecting enough of what they bill. Other times, they simply don't have enough work, or they are taking the wrong clients or cases. Discounting fees hurts, as well. If you offer a 15 percent discount for prompt payment, (1) you're assuming that the client won't pay timely without an incentive; and (2) you are dropping your revenues by 15 percent as well. So, your hours may look good, but a discount means that you aren't getting paid for all the time you worked. It also means that with less income, your overhead consumes a higher percentage of your earnings and impacts your firm's good health. You have to either bill more, collect more, or raise your rates to maintain your same level of gross profits when discounting. [See chart at the end of this chapter for a look at what a discount does to revenues.]

From there, I move to the timekeepers' productivity reports. Who is billing what, and how much are they collecting? I look to see if there are write-offs and write-downs that might be contributing to the problem. Then I get down to the nitty-gritty. How does everyone capture their time? Are their billing rates appropriate? Are their flat fees working for them?

If your overhead is taking an extra big bite out of your revenues, sit down with your calculator, your profit and loss statement, and your budget, and look for any particular line item that is unusually high. (You'll actually need your budgets and P&Ls from the past three years to get any sort of real feel for the appropriateness of your expenses.)

If you find numbers that seem to be unreasonable, find out what they represent. Two of my all-time favorite clients learned a valuable lesson when we looked at their numbers. Bob and Ray had been partners for only about two years when we met. Ray, the junior partner, was the businessman in the duo, while Bob was happy just practicing law and leaving the administrative stuff to Ray. Bob's former paralegal had been handling the bookkeeping duties for about 10 years.

Bob didn't have P&Ls from the past three years; however, he was able to produce several monthly statements (February, March, April, and June) from the previous year.

The two attorneys watched anxiously as I went over each statement carefully, comparing it to the others. There were two expense items, in particular, which stuck out. The phone expenses were:

February	$ 119.37
March	$ 137.25
April	$ 1,254.33
June	$ 128.98

"What happened in April to cause your phone expenses to run about $1,100 higher than usual?" I asked.

They looked at each other and shrugged. "We don't know," Ray replied.

I said, "Did you buy cell phones for everyone?"

"No."

"Did you invest in a new phone system for the office?"

"No."

"The amount isn't even a reasonable double payment. Every other month you've been down in the low $100s. So, you have no clue what this might be?"

"Nope," they replied.

I told them not to worry, we could figure it out by looking at the phone bills for these months. All charges would be detailed there.

They both looked sheepish and Bob said, "We don't have the phone bills. We don't want our bookkeeper to get overrun with paper, so after she pays a bill, she throws it away."

Two lessons in there actually: (1) question any expense that looks out of line at the time you first notice it; and (2) never throw away your old paid bills until you're past the IRS audit mark (typically, seven years).

The same went for the off-site storage charges. A large spike one month that wasn't an amount that would have been a double payment. Because it was for a store-it-yourself facility, there is no additional fee for file retrieval or anything like that. Again, they had no explanation, and admitted they hadn't ever paid much attention to their financial statements. They just filed them away in a drawer because they felt they should keep them "just in case."

Learn from Bob and Ray. Watch your expenses carefully each month. Watch for trends. Watch for unusual amounts. If you have someone else doing your books, review all bills before they are paid. Review your canceled checks and bank statements. It's always a good practice to have someone other than the person who prepares checks handle the bank reconciliation anyway. That person could be you.

I've just given you three ways to measure your firm's health, but there are many different measurements you can use. At a minimum, monitor the following on a regular basis:

- annual gross revenues;
- average number of hours billed per day;
- current fees charged;
- realization rates;
- effective rates;
- overhead-to-income percentage;
- number of new clients per month;
- the sources of new clients, the type of clients you receive from each source, the revenues generated from each of those clients;
- the costs and profitability of your various practice areas and/or services;
- the marketing costs per new client;
- turnover rate; and
- liquidity ratios.

Know where you are all the time. Whenever a new financial statement is generated, do your calculations and take your measurements. If something is out of line, attend to it immediately before it does harm to your practice. Ignorance may be bliss, but poverty stinks!

> *Tip: Give your firm a financial physical on a regular basis to keep it in good health!*

THE IMPACT OF A FEE DISCOUNT

RATE DISCOUNT

(% increase in revenues needed to maintain the same gross profit after a discount)

GROSS MARGIN

Amount of Discount	35%	40%	45%	50%	55%	60%
5%	16.67%	14.29%	12.50%	11.11%	10.00%	9.09%
10%	40.00%	33.33%	28.57%	25.00%	22.22%	20.00%
15%	75.00%	60.00%	50.00%	42.86%	37.50%	33.33%
20%	133.33%	100.00%	80.00%	66.67%	57.14%	50.00%

17

SELF-LIMITING BEHAVIORS:
HOW ATTORNEYS UNDEREARN

As a consultant to small law firms, I have discovered an unsettling phenomenon amongst the attorneys I meet. So many of these practitioners are struggling with chronic underearning, and I am at a complete loss to explain why. Simply put, ***underearning is earning below your potential***. Some of the symptoms of underearning include:

- not living the life you want;
- not being able to provide the lifestyle you would like for your family;
- not making enough money to cover your basic needs;
- not having enough money each month to be able to save for emergencies or retirement;
- not being able to give your staff the raises or bonuses they deserve;
- living in deprivation;
- not being able to do the things with the business that you would like; and
- constant stress about money.

Underearning is about making the choices that keep you earning below your potential. In his book, *Earn What You Deserve*, Jerrold Mundis tells us that underearning may take an active form or a passive form. ***Passive*** underearning is about choosing not to do something, or failing to do something that would have resulted in you making more money. Failing to raise your fees, refusing to spend money on software or equipment that would make you more efficient and productive, or not tending to your marketing are examples of passive underearning. ***Active*** underearning involves knowingly doing something that will cause you to underearn. Examples include: accepting a client whom you believe will not be able to pay your bills, providing excessive pro bono services, discounting your fees, writing off time, handling certain administrative (nonbillable) tasks yourself that could be outsourced (e.g., payroll and bookkeeping responsibilities, etc.).

Either consciously or unconsciously, too many attorneys are making the choices that cause them to underearn.

You are responsible for you.

Consider the stories of several solo practitioners. Each has a different set of issues, a different set of circumstances. You be the judge—who's an underearner and who isn't?

For the past 15 years, Sarah has been a solo practitioner with a lovely office suite in a wealthy community. With the help of her loyal, but frustrated, assistant, Sarah handles family law matters and does a few wills here and there. She is thousands of dollars in debt with credit cards and a line of credit. Sarah gives away hours of time each week because she "can't be bothered" making time entries for reading and responding to e-mails or chatting on the phone with clients. She offers free 30-minute initial consultations, but then loses control of the time and ends up spending one to two hours with each potential client. Sarah hates the idea of marketing, so her marketing plan consists of a small ad in the Yellow Pages and a one-page website. She much prefers to wait for her clients to refer others to her. She has never seen a profit and loss statement for her business, and has no interest in doing so. Sarah isn't overly worried about her financial problems because she knows she's the lone beneficiary of her 76-year-old Auntie Carole's estate and that money will more than settle her debts and get her back on her feet (providing Auntie Carole doesn't go into skilled nursing for the last few years of her life).

Is Sarah an underearner? Big time. Can you spot the self-limiting behaviors? How about these, for starters:

- fails to record all time worked (passive);
- consistently spends more time than planned in her free initial consultations (active);
- sends out client bills only 3-4 times per year (passive);
- writes off time (active);
- pays little to no attention to her firm's financial statements (passive);
- puts little effort into marketing to increase business (passive); and
- lives in hopes that someone else will get her out of her financial mess (passive).

Now, let's take a look at Roger's situation. While his issues differ from Sarah's, the end result is the same—underearning.

Roger has been in a small firm for most of his 23 years as an attorney. With a focus on business litigation, his practice is a nice complement to the practices of his two partners. Roger records all of his time meticulously every day. In fact, his time records are monuments to the art of timekeeping:

8:07-8:09	Read e-mail from client Jordan re settlement offer
8:09-8:14	Respond to client's e-mail
8:14-8:27	Coffee run
8:27-8:43	Review and sign motion in Smith case
8:43-8:48	Photocopy motion for forms file

If anyone could bill accurately and fairly for work performed, it would be Roger. He captures every minute of every day, so his billings should be maximized, right? One would think; however, Roger routinely writes down every client bill by about one-third of his time. It is apparently without conscious design (as far as the percentage of write down goes), but that's how it works out. Nearly every time entry on every bill shows some amount of "N/C" (no charge) time – usually 30-35 percent of each entry. In fact, his client bills look a lot like this:

2/9/09	Preparation for and meeting with opposing counsel to discuss the proposed sale of the laundromat to settle the debts of the parties to this matter; follow-up telephone conversation with client to provide an update on the status of her case; follow-up letter to opposing counsel confirming the agreement reached today during our meeting.	3.4 hrs (N/C 1.2 hrs)

Bill after bill after bill reflects this strange practice, an automatic write-down of each time entry, but always showing the client the actual time recorded, as well as the write-down. When asked the reasoning behind this, Roger replies, "I guess I just don't see the value of my work." With a stellar reputation in the local legal community, it is hard to understand why Roger doesn't have more self-confidence. His work is good, it is correct, it is timely, and it is responsive to his client's needs. He records every minute of his day, yet Roger is a chronic underearner. His self-limiting behaviors are crystal clear:

- not billing for all time worked;
- writing down time; and
- undervaluing his work.

Both Sarah and Roger are on the verge of destroying their practices. Sarah continues to complain about her financial woes, but thus far has been unwilling or unable to change her behavior to stop her pattern of underearning. She much prefers to wait for something or someone to save her (her clients to refer business, her boyfriend to marry and support her, a winning lottery ticket, Auntie Carole to catch a bad cold). Roger is more amenable to change, although at times he is merely going through the motions for the sake of the other partners in his firm. He still has difficulty believing he is worth his fee. Both attorneys are still hanging on by a thread. What a sacrifice! Their careers could have been quite different for both of them.

Don't be fooled by your income.

Now, let's look at Allan. His underearning isn't so easy to spot because he's making a decent living. Allan is a bankruptcy attorney with a good practice based on lots of referrals from past clients. He has three full-time employees to help him provide a superior level of customer service. Allan is well-thought-of in the local legal community, and he donates time to a legal clinic. Last year, Allan's firm grossed $425,000 and Allan took home about $115,000.

With a personal income of $115,000, how can Allan be classified as an underearner?

First, you need to remember the definition of an underearner: someone who is not earning at his/her potential.

Second, a peek at his aged accounts report will explain Allan's underearning. To attract clients, Allan advertises "payment plans available," and virtually every client accepts his offer. (I would, too!) He suggests a small amount each month, ranging anywhere from $25 to $100, depending on the client's general prospects. The problem is that these are bankruptcy clients, and all of their debts are about to be discharged. Allan doesn't exempt his fees because he claims, "My clients always honor their obligation to me."

With all due respect, they don't. Allan has more than 300 clients on his books who haven't made a payment in more than a year—many haven't sent money in several years. This means that although Allan charges $895 for a Chapter 7 bankruptcy, the clients who are delinquent have paid far less than that to achieve their freedom from debt.

Allan is guilty of both passive and active underearning. His passive underearning (not doing something which, in turn, causes him to underearn) is seen in his failure to collect his fee in full before beginning work, and failure to exempt his fees from his client's discharge of debts. Passive underearning also appears in his failure to pursue past-due accounts. Along with not getting paid in full, carrying excessively aged accounts on his books is costing him money in administrative expenses. Allan's active underearning is seen in his payment plan offer to people who are consulting with him because they have serious money issues. He is choosing to do something that has a high probability of causing him to underearn.

There are at least four steps Allan can take to stop the underearning:

1. He needs to accept only the clients who can pay his full fee up front. If they can't do it all at once, he might allow the client to divide the fee into several smaller payments over one or two months (all due before Allan will file the case with the court).

2. He must actively pursue his past-due accounts. He's got about $250,000 on the books in accounts receivable. Given his revenues, he shouldn't be carrying more than about $70,000-$75,000 in aged accounts. He's either got to get more aggressive with his collections policy, or he needs to write off the very old accounts, vow never to get into this situation again, and move on.

3. He must stop offering payment plans. Period. Think about it for a minute. If you needed to file for bankruptcy and had to come up with $895 for attorney's fees, I'm sure you could figure out a way to get the money. You could go to your parents for a loan, ask four friends to loan you $225 each, ask nine friends to loan you $100 each, sell back vacation or sick time to your employer, have a garage sale, sell some of the stuff you bought on credit on eBay, etc. Putting clients on payment plans isn't working for Allan, so he needs a different policy.

4. Allan needs to respect and care for his business. If he doesn't, who will?

Allan has made the choices that cause him to underearn. Now, it's time for Allan to choose to earn at his potential.

Sometimes it's okay to earn less.

Our last solo practitioner is Kay, an estate planning attorney. Kay gave birth to her first child early in the year and took two months off on maternity leave. Since then, she has been working only about 3.5 days a week to spend more time with the baby. Last year, Kay's practice grossed about $89,000, and she pocketed about $45,000.

From her numbers, you might assume that Kay is an underearner. Indeed, some might say that she isn't earning at her potential because she works part-time; however, let's take a closer look at Kay and her money.

Kay pays by the hour to share a legal assistant's time with another attorney on her floor. Her downtown office is located in a large suite, which is leased by her husband's employer. The boss cut her a terrific deal because he likes the idea of having an attorney handy, especially one who is also a notary public. Kay's overhead averages about 35 percent of revenues, so she runs a pretty tight ship. Probate is a small part of her practice, and she does bill hourly for that work (using an evergreen deposit account); however, most of her work (estate planning) is paid on a flat fee basis, and she never starts work until she's been paid in full. She's able to pay all of her office expenses, contribute to the family pot, fund her retirement plan to the maximum each year, save for the unforeseen, enjoy the lifestyle she wants, and spend precious time with her baby. Does Kay have the potential to make more money? Sure, but it would be at the expense of her preferred lifestyle. So, given her personalized business model, minimal overhead expenses, and all the circumstances of her life right now, Kay isn't underearning. She's meeting her needs at all levels.

Over the years, I have encountered a variety of behaviors that lead to underearning. Some are personal issues, while others are poor management strategies. Do any ring a bell with you?

- Failure to tend to the business side of the practice
- Giving away time
- Discounting fees
- Irregular billing
- Failure to market or relying on ineffective marketing strategies
- Accepting bad clients/cases
- Accepting clients who can't pay
- Lack of self-motivation
- Undervaluing your work
- Underbilling for work performed
- Write-offs
- Self-limiting beliefs
- A continuing expectation that someone or something will save you
- Rationalizing low income
- Lousy negotiating skills
- Reverse snobbery ("People with money aren't nice")
- Subtle self-sabotage
- Co-dependency (putting other people's needs ahead of your own)
- Living in financial chaos
- Lack of self-discipline
- Not working enough hours
- Filling free time with non-business activities and tasks (Internet surfing, computer games, endless chores, personal e-mails, shopping, and gazing out the window for long periods of time).

If you are an underearner, unless you understand how your behavior is taking money out of your pocket and those of your partners, you're going to have a hard time changing your behavior. Unless you see underearning as depriving your family of a better lifestyle, you aren't going to change. Unless you see underearning as earning below your potential—and recognize that you could be earning more—you will never believe that it doesn't have to be this way. Unless you get angry about it, you are not going to stop underearning.

Recognizing the signs of underearning.

Okay, so do you think you might be an underearner? Take a moment to answer the following questions and decide for yourself.

Circle the statements that apply to you, as well as those that might apply but you just aren't sure if they accurately describe you or not.

1. I often give away my services (pro bono work, not billing for all of the time worked, volunteering, answering questions for free on the telephone, free initial consultations, etc.)

2. My initial consultations almost always run over the time allotted, but I don't charge more for the extra time.

3. Raising my fees causes me such stress and fear that I only do it every few years.

4. I regularly discount my fees to encourage prompt payment.

5. Sometimes I feel that I'm not worth what I charge, so I write off part of my time.

6. I don't record my time contemporaneously for either hourly or flat fee work.

7. I let my accounts receivable become 90 days or more past due before I take action.

8. I continue working for clients who aren't paying me.

9. Talking with clients about money is uncomfortable for me.

10. I waive my advance fee deposit if a potential client can't afford it.

11. I have time management issues.

12. I am good at self-sabotage (accepting clients who are unable or unlikely to pay my fees, not setting goals and developing action plans to reach them, taking cases I'm not qualified to handle, billing irregularly, not doing focused marketing to attract my ideal client, etc.)

13. My debt level is high, I have very little in savings, my retirement account is underfunded, and I'm not clear on where my money goes.

14. I don't really know how much I actually earn until I see it on my tax return.

15. I continually put others' needs before my own.

16. I am often worried about money.

17. I fear for my financial future.

18. I believe that I can make money.

19. I am confident in the value of my services to my clients.

20. My expenses are always below my income.

21. Money is my friend and I appreciate what it does for me.

22. I believe I have a rosy financial future.

23. I experience very little fear or insecurity around money.

24. I am committed to getting paid what I am worth.

25. I love my work.

26. I am blessed with a supportive fan base (including spouse/partner, other family members, close friends, etc.)

27. I admire wealthy people.

28. I have little or no credit card debt.

29. I get myself in situations beyond my ability and then rise to them.

30. I am resilient and able to bounce back when I fail.

31. I am filled with gratitude for the success I've achieved.

32. I work very hard, but I know I don't have to do everything myself. I know how to delegate and set limits.

33. I am tenacious in achieving my goals.

34. I take action on past-due accounts as soon as they become delinquent.

35. I fire clients who don't pay me.

The dividing point in these questions is pretty obvious. If you answered "yes" to any of the first 17 questions, you probably are an underearner. A "yes" to questions 18-35 demonstrates that, even if you are underearning, you have a healthy relationship with money and a great chance of breaking that self-defeating pattern.

So, are you an underearner? Do you see that your underearning is a result of choices you make or actions you take or don't take?

Underearning — what's in it for you?

Why do you set yourself up to underearn? Any psychologist will tell you that we get something out of negative behavior, as well as positive. Underearning issues are frequently rooted in a lack of self-worth or a feeling of helplessness or hopelessness. What's behind your underearning?

When considering this issue, it's important to *remember the insidious damage caused by a long-term pattern of underearning.* It robs you of the peace that comes from knowing you are financially secure. Underearning seldom impacts only the underearner. Your pattern of underearning can:

- keep your practice partners from earning more;

- deprive you and your family of a lifestyle that could offer the activities, opportunities, and level of comfort you would all like to enjoy;

- restrict the growth of your practice;

- affect your ability to represent your clients to the best of your ability because you don't have the money to invest in the resources that would aid in representation;

- undermine your self-esteem and may even make you question your career choice;

- saddle you with constant worry about money that can distract you from your work; and

- cause you stress which can endanger your health by causing depression, anxiety, stress, sleeplessness, and over- or undereating.

In addition, underearners frequently feel guilty about not making as much money as they could.

Several years ago, I met an attorney who was the biggest underearner I had ever encountered. He prided himself on the fact that he drives a 40-year-old car. His home has no electricity. He works only about 1-2 hours a day and gives the rest of his time over to pro bono work. He has a wonderfully kind and caring heart, and pro bono work is his passion and his motivator. What he came to realize, though, is that this hippie-like lifestyle is *his* choice, not the choice of his eight-year-old daughter. She wants the things her friends have, and she wants to participate in the activities enjoyed by other eight-year-olds. His underearning no long affects only he and his wife; now, they have a child growing up in a life of deprivation. The problem is that his lifestyle is so ingrained in his psyche that he is terrified at the thought of giving it up and putting more emphasis on earning money. He has eschewed what he called the "superficial trappings" of mainstream America in favor of just getting by. It remains to be seen if he can make the change from chronic underearning to earning a sufficient amount to provide his family with some of the niceties of life—like an electric lamp.

How do you want to live out the rest of your career? What are you willing to do to achieve that?

If you suspect your pattern of underearning is rooted somewhere deep inside, search out a therapist who deals specifically with money and/or esteem issues, or a certified financial recovery coach to help you break out of your self-limiting practices. It may not be easy to change the behaviors that are keeping you from earning at your potential, but the end result will be well worth the effort. You've worked hard to get where you are, and being able to make enough money to take care of yourself and your family is one of your rewards. You deserve it!

> *Tip:* **If your choices have caused you to earn below your potential, make the choice to change that behavior and start earning what you are worth!**

18

YOUR INCOME:
WHAT IS ENOUGH?

When an attorney calls me for help, the conversation nearly always starts with "I'm not making enough money." The caller usually goes on to assure me that she is working as hard as she can, he is good about capturing all of his billable time, overhead is as low as it can get, but, "There just never seems to be enough money."

My question to the attorney is simple, "What is enough?"

The replies are all over the place, but the theme is the same:

"I don't know, but this isn't it."

"I want to be able to give my family a nice lifestyle."

"I want to be able to take more time off and travel more."

"I want to cover my office expenses and still be able to take a comfortable amount from the business for myself."

"I'd like to cover my basic needs, but still be able to have dinner with friends once in awhile, or buy a new dress, or get season tickets to the symphony."

"'Enough' means that I can pay cash for a new set of tires."

"'Enough' will take away the stress I constantly feel about money."

While all valid goals, I still don't know what "enough" is for these attorneys. How about you? Is there a magic number that defines "enough" for you? I have found there to be a direct correlation between an attorney's ability to articulate financial goals and his success rate in reaching those goals.

Come out of the money fog.

In her terrific book, *Earning What You're Worth: Why Women Underearn*, Mikelann Valterra refers to the vagueness around money as "the money fog." I see it all the time in small law firms; attorneys unable to answer basic questions about the firm's finances, or attorneys unclear on where their money goes. Attorneys unable to tell me how much they have to bill and collect each month to break even. I see attorneys abdicating responsibility for the firm's financial management to a bookkeeper or even a staff person doing double duty, or attorneys with no definite financial goals. Attorneys dissatisfied with their income, yet unable to define what would be satisfactory.

Chris was proud of the fact that she had billed an all-time high of just over $24,000 for the previous month. This was about $5,700 more than her previous all-time high. Chris's average monthly billings run about $13,500–$15,000. Billing $24,000 should have put Chris on Easy Street; however, in reality, Chris had gone to her parents once again for yet another loan. When asked, Chris said that her personal living expenses are "minimal," but that she tries to pay herself about $5,000 a month. Chris also describes her office rent as "very low," and her overhead as "manageable." According to Chris, routinely billing in the $13,500–$15,000 range should cover her overhead and allow her to pay herself as planned. Unfortunately, it wasn't working that way. In the previous five months, her monthly take ranged from a low of $1,800 to a high of $4,350.

So, what's wrong with Chris's practice?

Chris is living in a money fog. The first tip-off comes from her responses to questions about money. Using words like "minimal," "very low," or "manageable" may be reassuring to Chris, but they don't help her understand her financial needs. They are vague and don't represent real dollar amounts.

Living in a money fog almost guarantees that you will not enjoy the level of success you seek. Until you can get a handle on your personal and business finances, you're going to have trouble. You need to understand your money; where it goes, how you get it, how much you need, what you have to spend to make more money, how much belongs to you and how much to your firm, how you'll cover emergencies, and so on.

For the moment, let's start with "enough".

So, what is enough?

Simply put, having "enough" means that you are able to provide for your:

- basic needs;
- wants/desires; and
- savings.

[You'll note that taxes are not included in this list as a separate item. Consider your obligation to your loving Uncle Sam as being a basic need. If you cross him, he can get ugly; so, your basic need here is to pay up and stay on his good side.]

"Wants/desires" include the treats, travel, and dresses mentioned above. This is the category that provides the fun and rewards in our lives.

"Savings" would include both your emergency fund and the money you are putting aside for retirement. This category provides us with a sense of safety and security.

Now, what is enough for you? How much money do you need each month to meet your basic needs, cover your wants/desires, and allow you to add to your savings?

The "Customized Cash Flow Plan" at the end of this chapter will help you determine what you need to bring in each month to cover your routine expenses and savings. As you fill in the blanks, please use real numbers – not "I think . . ." or "I'd like to spend . . ." figures. Go back through your check register and paid-bills file to get actual amounts for the items listed. If you don't currently spend money on some of these items, but hope to when you make more money, don't enter an amount here. This will come later when you prepare your personal budget.

Under the "Savings" section, think of everything you need to save for. Are you facing college expenses for a child in the coming years? Do you plan to leave the practice of law feet first, or do you actually hope to retire one day? Would you like to be able to build your dream home? Buy a hot red sports car? Enjoy an exotic adventure vacation in the Amazon jungles? Take six months off work? Or be like the attorney who aspires to pay cash for a set of tires? Here's where you'll want to combine what you *need* to save each month with what you *want* to save.

Once you've completed the plan, divide the total expenses by 12 to determine what you need to bring in each month to cover your basic needs. Remember, this only shows personal basic needs, not any expenses related to the operation of your small firm. We're just getting a handle on what your compensation must be to take care of your personal life.

Were there any surprises? Anything you can cut back on? Anything you should be paying now, but aren't? It's a good idea to revisit this earning plan on an annual basis to just make sure that you clearly understand your financial needs.

Now that you know the minimum amount of money you need to earn each month to meet your basic needs, it's time to figure out the additional money you need to generate to provide yourself and your family with the lifestyle you desire. Because these items come out of your discretionary cash, you'll prepare a budget of projected expenses, rather than look at historical data. Among the items you might include would be:

- Vacation/holiday travel
- Gift giving
- Charitable giving
- Entertainment
- Self-enrichment lessons/classes
- Hobbies
- Outdoor activities (golf, windsurfing, kayaking, etc.)
- Lattes (although in Seattle, we call this a "basic need")
- Hair extensions/tattoos/other personal enhancements
- Collections
- Spa services
- A motorcycle/boat/airplane/snowmobile/horse
- Country club membership
- Wine club

You get the idea. All right, maybe a tattoo isn't for you, but think about what would add pleasure and enhance the quality of your life. What brings you joy? What makes you feel special? What is your reward of choice when you do a good job?

Once you've completed your plan, you will have a quantified goal—an actual dollar amount that you need to earn each month. No more vagueness; now you know what "enough" looks like!

It's much easier to develop a plan to reach your goals when you know what your goals are. You'll use this information in setting your billing rates. You'll refer to your cash flow plan in developing your business plan and your marketing strategies. What do you need to do to achieve your financial goals? What business decisions will help you get there? Incorporate your personal financial needs into your business financial needs to make sure both you and your practice are financially secure.

Come out of the money fog, identify your needs, and build a practice that will provide you with "enough".

> *Tip: Before you can have enough, you need to know what enough is!*

CASH FLOW EVALUATION

INCOME	Current	Sub-totals
Salary		
Self-employment		
Rental income 1		
Rental income 2		
Gifts		
Social Security		
Pension		
Other		
GRAND TOTAL INCOME	$0.00	

EXPENSES

Rent		$0.00

Loans

Mortgage		
Home equity line/loan		
Car loan		
Student loans		
Personal loan		$0.00

Credit card monthly payments

Credit card 1 (Name here)		
Credit card 2 (Name here)		
Credit card 3 (Name here)		
Credit card 4 (Name here)		
ATM Fees; late fees; bank fees		$0.00

Food

Groceries (incl. liquor/cigarettes)		
Dinners out		
Lunches out		
Breakfasts out		
Snacks/lattes/bakery at work; en route etc.		$0.00

Entertainment

Cable TV		
DSL/Broadband/etc.		

Movies/popcorn		
CDs/DVDs		
Books		
Subscriptions/newspapers		
Concerts/events/sports		
Sports-fitness		
Hobbies - gardening, collections,		
Other (home entertainment, etc.)		
Clothing (work, leisure, sports, vacation, etc.)		
Dues		$0.00

Personal care

Hair salon/spa		
Coaching/therapy/workshops/classes		
Massage/acupuncture/health club, etc.		
Eye glasses/contacts, etc.		
Housecleaning service		
Laundry/dry cleaning		
Cosmetics/toiletries		$0.00

Car

Gas		
Registration		
Repair/tires/brakes/etc.		
Service - oil/filters/etc.		
Parking/tickets		
Car insurance		$0.00

Phone service

Home phone		
Cell phone		$0.00

Utilities

Electric		
Gas		
Water/garbage		
Other		$0.00
Transportation (bus, taxis, etc.)		
Travel/vacations/souvenirs		

Home improvements - large (remodeling, roof, painting, etc.)		
Home maintenance - small (rug cleaning, furnace maintenance, gardening, sm items)		
Gifts - charity		
Gifts - others		$0.00
Insurance		
Home		
Umbrella		
Medical		
Dental		
Life		
Disability		
Long term care		$0.00
Medical, Dental, Eye		
Co-pays - medical		
Dental care		
Drugs/prescriptions/vitamins, etc.		
Opthamologist/optometrist		
Other		
Sundries/Miscellaneous - postage, cards, knickknacks, stationery		
Dependant care/family assistance		
Pet expenses (food, vet, rooming, etc.)		$0.00
Savings		
Short term savings		
Retirement savings		
College/education savings		
Vacations/holiday savings		$0.00
Taxes		
Real estate taxes		
IRS taxes		$0.00
GRAND TOTAL EXPENSES	$0.00	
POSITIVE (OR NEGATIVE) CASH FLOW	**Total Inc less Total Exp)**	**$0.00**

19

UNTRUTHS ATTORNEYS TELL THEMSELVES:
HOW THEY HURT THE BUSINESS

Ever hear a little voice in your head? Come on, admit it, you have. It's a tiny voice, but sometimes its message is deafening. This voice spews out untruths. You know, things such as:

"I don't deserve success."

"I'm not worth what I charge."

"Someday someone is going to find out that I'm a fraud."

"If I just work harder, I'll make more money."

And, that's just the beginning. Feel free to add your own inner voice's big fat lies to the list. Call it what you will, this voice is not that of a trusted friend—it's the voice of fear, doubt, insecurity, and deception. You know the voice. We've all heard it at one time or another. Isn't it uncanny how your inner voice can go right to the core of your insecurities? It's almost like it can read your mind!

If left uncontrolled, this little voice can torpedo your plans, scuttle your practice, and shipwreck your dreams. I'm no psychologist, but I can usually recognize the unfounded beliefs of my clients early on in our work. Once they release themselves from the stranglehold of these untruths, they can get on with being successful.

Let's take a closer look at some of the untruths attorneys tell themselves. We'll start with one of my favorites . . .

If I just work harder, I'll make more money.

Makes sense, doesn't it? The harder you work, the more money you'll make.

Perhaps. The thing is, however, that I've rarely found a small firm practitioner who could work much harder. They are usually just about topped out as it is.

When an attorney phones me for help, without exception, it's because the lawyer isn't making enough money, or he isn't where he thought he'd be at this point in his career, or she's looking at retirement in seven years and has realized that she is financially unprepared to quit work.

In some cases, they've already tried working harder, and it hasn't gotten them where they expected it would. That's because, for small firm practitioners, making more money is rarely about working harder—it's about working smarter. Increasing efficiency and productivity, managing the firm's resources more effectively, closely monitoring cash flow, keeping on top of past-due accounts, targeted marketing to attract ideal clients, outsourcing or delegating nonrevenue-producing tasks to a lower-paid employee—these are all factors that can increase profitability. Working harder? Not so much.

If you want to make more money, giving up evenings and weekends is not the answer. Start by paying closer attention to your business.

I have to do it myself because I can't afford to hire help.

How often do you end up making photocopies, driving to Office Depot for supplies, handling research that a skilled paralegal could do, or struggling with your bookkeeping software in an effort to keep your ledger current?

And, your reason is . . .?

Okay, if you are a solo practitioner with no staff, I can understand your argument that there isn't anyone else to handle these tasks. I don't necessarily buy it, but I can understand it.

If you are doing clerical work, are you billing your client for that time? Probably not. Doing the clerical stuff cuts into your potential billable time. Let me give you a real-life example.

Patty is a solo practitioner with an office at the edge of a major city's business district. She loves the proximity to the courts, post office, bank, and office supply superstore. She visits the post office (a five-minute drive, once she's retrieved her car from the parking lot in the next block) three to five times a week to send Express Mail packages to her clients.

Patty makes the bank runs, treks to the office supply store for a ream of paper when she runs out, and trots back to her office if she discovers she's missing a document when she gets to court. To her way of thinking, she's in an ideal location.

Patty also has a part-time assistant who comes in one day a week. Patty explains, "I'd love to have Abby work more, but I just can't afford it."

And, she's right. Patty spends so much time performing nonrevenue-producing clerical tasks that her potential billable hours are significantly reduced.

Patty agreed to take my 30-day challenge to see exactly where all of her time goes. She agreed to log everything she did during the day, each day. Didn't matter if it was client-related or not—just record everything.

At the end of the 30 days, Patty was astonished to find that she was spending:

- five to eight hours per week on bookkeeping tasks, paying bills, preparing client bills, and making bank runs;

- four to six hours per week going to and from the post office. During the holiday season, one trip to the post office alone took an hour and 45 minutes;

- an hour or more per week going to/from the office supply store (highlighted by a recent emergency trip when she ran out of paper while printing out a document for a client who was coming to sign in about an hour);

- approximately two to three hours per week photocopying and preparing mailings; and

- another two hours per week handling the janitorial duties in her office to save money.

While Patty didn't make a dash back to the office, she did get to court with an important document missing from her file because Abby couldn't always get to the filing on her one day in the office.

The log revealed other instances of lost billable time, as well. So was it really easier and more cost-effective for Patty to continue to handle these clerical tasks herself? Let's do the math.

Patty's billing rate is $175/hr. If we say, conservatively, that Patty spends 15 hours per week on clerical tasks that would represent a potential loss of billings of $2,625 for the week. Patty pays Abby $22/hr, or $176/day. If Abby worked an extra day each week, and her assistance allowed Patty to bill just one more hour per week, it would cost Patty only $1 out-of-pocket. More to the point, Patty would have had eight additional hours of help during the week, and that has to translate to more than just one additional hour of billable time for Patty.

If you don't identify with Patty's situation, perhaps solo practitioner John's predicament will ring a bell.

Despite my advice to turn over his payroll function to an outside payroll service, John chose to have his untrained (and protesting) paralegal assume payroll duties on a brand new software program that neither of them understood. "I can't afford $85 a month to have someone figure out payroll for only four employees," he proclaimed.

Payroll and taxes are two areas where you don't want to make mistakes. John's thriftiness came back to bite him 10 months later when he was the subject of a random audit by the State Department of Labor. The auditor found numerous mistakes in calculating overtime pay for his hourly paid employees. The result? A hefty fine (well into four figures) and back pay to his underpaid employees. Let's see, 10 months x $85 = $765 for the payroll service versus a penalty of several thousand dollars. I'm not sure he made the right call, are you?

If you have a task or function in your practice that could benefit from new technology, outside help, or additional training, arguing that you can't afford to get help doesn't hold water. If assistance will help increase productivity, relieve you of tasks to which you are not well-suited or that are nonrevenue-producing, or can better be handled by someone specifically trained to the task, find the money somewhere. You'll make it up and then some in the long run by putting your time to a better use— producing billable work.

I'm too busy to market now.

Congratulations! What an enviable position in which to find yourself. Thank goodness, you'll never lose a client and your current work will never end.

Perhaps you'll find the story of the 14-attorney Emerson & Francis Law Firm of interest. Not particularly adept at marketing the firm in the first place, the attorneys excused their lack of marketing activities by pointing to the two labor-intensive cases they had been working on for the last one-and-a-half years. Everyone in the firm was logging long hours in preparing for Client Sherrie's upcoming trial. (One of the paralegals alone racked up 86 hours in overtime during a two-week period.) Each month huge bills were going out and huge checks were coming in. These practitioners were living every attorney's dream—two clients with seemingly bottomless pockets. Then the crafty client opposing Sherrie did the unthinkable; he offered a hefty sum to settle the matter, and Sherrie accepted. After a little wind-up work, the case was over, and Sherrie stopped sending the huge checks.

No worries, however, because Client Donna's case was heating up and she was pushing the firm to take her matter to trial. While she complained about the large monthly bills, she still paid them. The Emerson & Francis attorneys knew there was a very strong chance that Donna was going to lose if she went to trial, and they advised her to settle; however, they also knew that if she did, the legal work would end—and so would those fat checks. And, that's just what happened. Donna settled, refused to pay the firm's last statement, and told them she had paid them enough already, especially in light of the fact that she didn't get what she wanted in the end—satisfaction in court.

The firm struggled along with the remaining small matters they were handling for other clients, and tried to get the attorneys revved up about marketing. Over the course of the next nine months, the firm was forced to cut loose half of its staff, more than half of its attorneys, and its out-of-state branch office. Eventually, it folded. ***Waiting to market until you have plenty of time to do it just might be too late.***

I'm not worth what I charge.

Says who? Oh, yeah, I forgot—you! Have your clients ever told you that you aren't worth what you charge? If you answered "yes" to the last question, skip straight to the rest of this book and learn how to turn that around. If you answered "no," then listen up.

You may be thinking you aren't worth the money because the work is easy for you. If you've seen one estate plan, you've seen them all. You could put together a will in your sleep. Got a client who wants to file for bankruptcy? He hardly needs you because it's all just forms that anyone could fill out.

Let's consider how a professional in another service industry handles this. We'll look at the case of Jerry's handyman, Ted. Jerry was thrilled that he was able to purchase a 19th century farmhouse for an amount significantly below his budget. Now, Jerry would have plenty of money for the rehab he was planning to do on the charming old building.

Months later, the workmen were gone, the furniture was in place, and Jerry would have really been enjoying his new life in the country, if it weren't for that darned squeaking floor in the front parlor. Jerry tried everything he could think of to quiet the squeak, but no luck. He even solicited suggestions from the regulars at the local hardware store, but still the floor squeaked.

Finally, he followed his neighbor's tip and called in Ted, the handyman. When Ted arrived, Jerry took him through to the front parlor and did a little jig over the squeaky spot so Ted could more fully understand his frustration. Ted thoughtfully considered the situation, then opened up his toolbox, removed his hammer and a nail, and crossed the floor to where Jerry was standing. Kneeling, Ted positioned the nail, and pounded it into the beautiful oak floor with four good whacks.

As Ted was replacing his hammer in his toolbox, Jerry did his dance again – and no squeak. He was ecstatic! As he turned with a broad smile, Ted handed him his bill. Jerry's smile quickly faded when he saw that Ted was charging him $50 for this job. On the bill, Ted had written:

Hammering the nail: $3

Knowing where to put the nail: $47

You went through how many years of law school and have practiced how long to be able to do what you do? Some of the things you do may not seem like much to you, but they bring tremendous value to your clients because they solve problems, facilitate an action, make things easier for them, give them peace of mind and a sense of security, get them out of trouble, or lessen the consequences of poor judgment.

So, while you may not believe you're worth the money, unless your clients tell you so, they feel otherwise. Believe them—they aren't lying to you.

I'm smart—I should be able to manage my practice.

You are smart. You completed 19 years of school, graduated law school, and passed the bar; but, if you already know everything there is to know about how to successfully manage your practice, you probably wouldn't be reading this book. The first thing you have to do is get past your belief (if you still have it) that law school prepared you to be the complete lawyer—able to both practice law and manage your practice. It didn't. For the most part, you didn't get the training you need to successfully manage your business as a solo or small firm practitioner.

The good news is there is help available. The American Bar Association, as well as state and local bar associations, offer a variety of continuing legal education programs dealing with law practice management issues. State bar associations now offer law office management assistance programs, or something similar, which are great resources for solo and small firm practitioners. Most have lending libraries that allow you to access the wisdom of those who have already figured out what you are still trying to unravel. Many of these bar departments have popular software programs available to test drive on bar computers. What a great way to kick the tires before writing the check.

I want you to remember this: you are smart, and you can run a successful law practice. You just might need to work on your management techniques and strategies a bit more to be able to build the practice of your dreams, but you can do it!

Someday someone is going to find out that I'm a fraud.

I don't know a self-employed person who hasn't held this fear at one time or another. My sense is that we are more likely to doubt our wisdom, our skills, and our abilities when we're on our own because we don't get feedback from supervisors and co-workers. You may not realize how important it is to receive validation in the workplace, but we all crave it. And, frequently it's missing in a small firm (especially when you're the boss with no one over you).

Start a rainy-day file for yourself. Add in any notes or letters of appreciation that you receive. Print out any e-mails that say thank you in a meaningful way. Ask your clients what they like best about working with you. Save the evaluations when you speak at a CLE. Put only positive things in this file—things that make you feel better when you read them. Then, pull your file out on rainy days—it doesn't have to be raining literally, but, those days when the self-doubt really sets in. (I live in Seattle, and we have so many rainy days that I've nearly worn my file out.) I keep one particular CLE evaluation taped above my desk. Out of all the speakers that day, the attorney wrote only one word on her evaluation. After my name, she wrote, "Perfect!" That never fails to make me feel better!

Self-doubt is fairly common. The trick is not to let it take over your life. Replace those negative thoughts with memories of that terrific closing argument you gave that won your client's case, or the special needs trust you crafted for the parents of a disabled child, or the adoption you facilitated for the childless couple, or the large judgment you received on behalf of your severely injured client, or the divorce and restraining order you obtained for a victim of domestic abuse. You've got a treasure trove of memories that refute this untruth of self-doubt many times over. Dig them out once in awhile and remind yourself just how terrific you are!

We all hear that little voice from time to time. Sometimes it sounds remarkably like our parent's voice; sometimes it's the voice of a childhood teacher, or the school bully. It's just a little voice. It can't harm you unless you let it, and I don't want you to listen to it. Replace wrong thinking with right thinking and see where it takes you.

> *Tip: "... and the truth shall set you free!"*

20

SOMETIMES THE PROBLEM IS YOU:
PERSONAL HABITS THAT HURT

We've all got them—those little quirks and habits that accompany us wherever we go. While some of these characteristics can actually be quite charming, others get in the way of our success by hindering productivity (and, in turn, potential billings). What's that you say? "Not me?" Just to make sure you're clean, please take a moment to consider some of the personal habits that can hurt your practice.

Procrastination.

Procrastination reduces productivity, adds stress for you and your staff, and robs you of revenues. Consider the case of Peter, the procrastinating practitioner. Peter seems to get some sort of thrill out of resolving last-minute crises, usually brought on by his procrastination. Peter never walks out of his office—he explodes. He throws his door wide open, bursts forth into the hallway and grabs anyone who happens to be close by. "Fax this to Attorney Y" or "Make six copies of this document and get it to the courthouse within the next 30 minutes," he commands. Doesn't matter if the person whose help he is enlisting is the receptionist or another attorney in his firm, everyone is expected to pull together to handle his crisis. In addition, Peter frequently signs final documents without reading them. His oft-stated rationale is, "We've just got to get this out the door and to the court fast. If it's not right, we'll file an amended version tomorrow."

When things settle down and the document is safely on its way to court, Peter sighs in relief and says, "Great work, gang. We really pulled this one out of the fire."

Ultimately, the work product that goes out is not his best work; indeed, at times it's not even adequate. Peter is pleased because he beat the deadline once again, and he tells himself that the quality of the work is the best he could do "in the time available." (Never mind that Peter's clients are paying for and deserve better than adequate work.)

Unfortunately, this is Peter's standard mode of operation. It's a rare occasion when work is handled any other way than in a gut-wrenching panic. Peter's paralegal has developed TMJ since beginning work with him. The receptionist is now on antidepressants and is frequently absent from work with migraine headaches. An associate was pressed into service on Peter's crises so many times last year that his own work suffered and the firm gave him an annual bonus that was significantly less than his peers received.

What Peter doesn't realize is that his procrastination is costing the firm dearly in several ways:

- The quality of the work suffers and his clients are sometimes unhappy with his slipshod work product. No law practice can afford to have dissatisfied clients.

- Clients don't like to be overbilled; on the other hand, they don't want a low bill at the expense of the quality and effectiveness of the attorney's work—and they certainly don't want to be billed for a "redo" of faulty work that was sent out in haste.

- Staff turnover is high (no one seems to last more than a few months) and turnover takes a big bite out of the bottom line.

- Some of the other firm attorneys are angry because their work gets bumped to accommodate Peter's big, adrenalin-pumping emergency.

- The firm's reputation with the court suffers because court personnel complain about Peter all the time. The last-minute crunches frazzle the court staff, as well.

- Peter can only bill for work he actually performs on behalf of a client; so, by squeezing a six-hour project into only 90 minutes, Peter is not only short-changing his client with a shoddy work product, but he's also short-changing his firm of potential revenue.

Beyond this, an ethical question arises: did Peter serve his client to the best of his ability? Did he represent his client conscientiously, competently, ardently, and with diligence? Did the client receive value for his money? Given the fact that Peter sometimes must file an amended document to correct a flawed document, one could, arguably, assume that Peter does not serve his client well in all instances.

How about you? Are you a procrastinator? Is your bad habit hurting your practice? Make your clients happy by doing the job they deserve, make your employees happy by giving them ample lead time to accomplish their work, feel better about your work by spending the time necessary to produce quality work, and just maybe you'll make more money, as well.

Clutter and disorganization.

"Research indicates that people waste an hour or more each day searching for lost items or working in ways that are not productive," says Standolyn Robertson, President of the National Association of Professional Organizers. There are roughly 230 workdays each year. An attorney who spends 15 minutes a day looking for lost files, trying to find the draft of a document, or searching for a misplaced phone message loses about 58 billable hours per year. At $200/ hr, that's an annual loss of $11,600 per year!

How much time do you spend each day looking for things in your office? Do the math. Clutter and disorganization are costing you.

If you're not organized, don't expect a staff person to be able to shape you up. No one can organize *you* except *you* (with help). If disorganization is a problem for you, seek the help of a professional organizer. These fine folks can help you develop a work environment that is healthy, supportive, calming, and functional. For your clients' sake, commit to getting your office organized. They need your full attention on their work, not on trying to find an elusive piece of paper or the check they sent last week.

Think you can't afford it? Think about that lost $11,600 each year. A few hours with a professional organizer can add thousands of dollars to your bottom line. Money well spent, I'd say.

Poor time management/poor planning.

Several years ago, I was working with Glenda, an attorney who wasn't making enough money (her words, and I agreed). Through my interviews with both Glenda and her legal assistant, I discovered that Glenda didn't spend much time each day on revenue-producing work. Most of her paying work was under her county contract, which paid about $165 per criminal defense case (start to finish). So even when Glenda did work for those clients, it gained her next to nothing. Glenda was quite forthcoming about the problem. She said she was under tremendous stress because of lack of money, so she played computer games to relieve the stress. By her own account, she was spending up to six hours a day on Free Cell. Now, that's a lot of stress to relieve!

I suspected that Glenda's computer gaming had less to do with stress and more to do with time management skills. While it would seem on the surface that she was procrastinating, I believed Glenda was simply mismanaging her time. Glenda complained frequently that she didn't know:

- what to work on next;
- how to schedule work time;
- how to start the project;

- how to prioritize her tasks;

- the next step to take to move the project along;

- how to use small blocks of time effectively; and

- how to limit interruptions.

So, Free Cell won out. Not surprisingly, my first recommendation was that Glenda delete the "Games" folder from the computer. Old habits are hard to break, and in the end, she couldn't do it.

I wish I could report that Glenda was able to save her practice, but it was too late. Lacking the time management skills to help her handle her work and get sufficient money coming in, Glenda was forced to close her practice. She's now doing contract work for other attorneys, one project at a time. She certainly still has some of the same time management problems, but being accountable to another attorney for specific deadlines has helped her make better decisions about how to prioritize her time and tasks.

Attorneys doing too much clerical work.

Practitioners who spend time making photocopies, sending faxes, ordering office supplies, or stuffing envelopes, etc., are cutting into both productivity and profitability. Few attorneys would feel right about charging a client for time spent making photocopies, as an example. While the argument that, "It's faster if I just do it," may be true, the lost billable time will almost always outweigh the speed factor. When in doubt about what to do next, ask yourself the number one time-management question: "What is the best use of my time right now?" You wouldn't expect to hear an attorney respond, "Doing clerical work." Let your staff handle the clerical tasks. That's what you pay them to do, and the reason is to free you to do the billable work.

Don't have staff? Consider retaining the services of a virtual assistant to handle clerical duties. Through the use of technology, attorneys and staff don't even have to be in the same state anymore. Increase profitability by making the best use of your time. Skip the clerical work in favor of billable work.

Not preparing for the unexpected.

Running a law practice without a Plan B is akin to skydiving without a backup parachute. If your main chute doesn't open properly, you've got a bigger problem than even Houston can help with. In a law firm, Plan B would include:

- daily backup of your computer system;

- an attorney(s) who can fill in during your absence (vacation, illness, incapacitation, etc.);

- an emergency fund to cover an economic downturn, your inability to work for a period of time, unexpected expenses, a unique business opportunity, etc.;

- a disaster recovery plan; and

- a roster of technology experts to help you get up and running when you have a system crash.

As TV journalist Anderson Cooper noted of the lack of preparations made by the city of New Orleans before Hurricane Katrina hit, "Hope is not a plan." Hoping that nothing goes wrong is of no help when something does go wrong. And, rest assured, it will.

I guess it's human nature, but an amazing number of attorneys live in a state of denial. As I write this book, the U.S. is in the worst economic crisis of my lifetime. Banks are collapsing, credit has dried up, thousands of homeowners are facing foreclosure, and massive layoffs seem to be a staple of the nightly news broadcasts. Six months ago, attorney after attorney would tell me, with a smug little smile, that his or her practice is bulletproof. They said that legal services will always be in demand, people will always sue other people, unhappy couples will always want divorces, and everyone wants to have a current will in place for peace of mind. I believed differently. In fact, I offered a seminar entitled "Survival Tips: How to Protect Your Firm and Get Paid in Uncertain Times"—and no one came.

Funny what a difference a few months can make. Reality has cast a bright light on the foolishness of denial, and attorneys across the country are fighting for survival right now. Clients are taking longer to pay their bills, some are refusing to provide an advance fee deposit before representation begins, still others have asked to have their deposits refunded because they need the money. Law firms that were operating on a fairly narrow profit margin before the Wall Street crash are now scrambling to stay afloat. Small firms with good credit standings have been notified of significant decreases in their available lines of credit. In case of emergency, they don't have access to the funds they've tapped into in the past. I fear for the future of some of these firms.

Failure to plan for the unexpected can result in the demise of your firm. Conduct a worst-case scenario audit of your practice to help you identify where you need to do some strategizing. Name every possible negative-impact occurrence you and your staff can think of. Your list might include earthquake, hurricane, flooding, power outage, police activity, civil disturbance, hazardous materials spill in your office building or neighborhood, a bridge out or major road to the office closed, injury or death of attorney or employee, and so on. What are your weak spots? Make developing your Plan B a priority. Once you've got it down on paper, review it regularly for its continuing applicability. *Failure to plan is a plan for failure*. Remember the Boy Scouts—"Be prepared."

Inattention to law firm metrics.

As a solo or small firm practitioner, ignorance of your firm's financial situation can prove fatal to your practice. Lack of attention to your firm's metrics will absolutely keep you from maximizing your success. Instead, make business decisions based on factual data, rather than assumptions. Beef up your use of the marketing strategies that generate the most profitable new work for you. Know what's working and what's not working in your management style. Learn all you can about your firm's financial situation. Listen to its rhythm, what makes it hum, what causes disruption.

I had lunch this week with Tom, a partner in a 4-partner, 18-associate law firm. I asked how many people worked in his firm, and he didn't have a clue. I asked which of the firm's practice areas is most profitable. He replied, "I don't have any idea." I asked what percent of revenues went to overhead, and he said, "I don't know." I asked how much they still owe on their building remodel loan, and he replied, "I don't really care. We'll just keep paying until the bank says to stop sending money."

Ignorance may be bliss, but it's not a sound management strategy. Make it your business to get to know your business from the inside out.

Ineffective supervision of staff.

Your staff is your most valuable asset, but it's not going to be the best it can be without strong leadership. Start on Day 1 with a discussion of what your staff can and cannot do as law firm employees. Stress confidentiality, honesty, integrity, care and compassion for your clients, the importance of error-free work and careful attention to the smallest details of their work.

As the lawyer, you are ethically and professionally responsible for all that your staff does in your name. Ethical violations amongst staff members occur when attorneys are not paying close attention to what's happening under their very noses. From the bookkeeper who embezzles thousands of dollars from the firm's accounts, to the receptionist who regularly discusses the more salient aspects of your clients' cases over the dinner table with her family, you are responsible. Don't assume that employees who have previous law firm experience know the ethical dos and don'ts of law firm employment. You don't know what they learned at another job. Just as children learn from watching their parents, employees learn how to act from watching their attorney bosses. Do yourself a favor and lay down your expectations up front, then reinforce them from time to time through staff meetings, one-on-one counseling, etc.

Beyond the ethical issues, you need to supervise your staff's work. Monitor the quality of the work product, make sure even routine tasks are being handled timely and appropriately, address behavioral problems quickly and with an eye to salvaging the employee. Know what goes on in your office, and how it impacts you and your clients.

Remember that you are ultimately responsible for any malfeasance of your employees. Attorneys have been disbarred for the actions of a staff member. Don't let that happen to you.

Timewasters.

Quick, name your top three office timewasters. Mine are computer games, cats (I work at home), and friends who call for a personal chat during my business day.

While the actual timewasters are as varied as the individuals shackled to them, they all have one thing in common: they rob us of productivity and money! Every six minutes I spend playing computer mahjong is 0.1 hr that I cannot bill. Every 30-minute personal telephone call is 0.5 hr that I don't have to put into a billable task.

To determine what your timewasters are, take the 30-day challenge. Write down everything you do and the amount of time you spent doing it. Write down every trip to the coffee machine, your lunch hour, computer game session, billable time—every minute of every day. At the end of 30 days, you're going to be surprised to see where your time really goes. The biggest shock will be how much time was lost to what can only be described as timewasters. Identify them and get rid of them. Be ruthless. They are costing you.

If you are addicted to computer games, delete them from the computer. If you have a candy dish at your desk, cut down on interruptions by moving it to the lobby or coffee area. If coworkers or employees continually interrupt your work, close your door. If e-mails consume hours of your day, limit yourself to checking your in-box only two or three times each day at preset times. Then, limit how much time you'll allow yourself to read and reply to messages. Select only the client-related e-mails for immediate attention. If a client requests you to take action on something, add that request to your to-do list, along with your other tasks. Treat e-mail as you would correspondence received in the mail. As an example, when you receive a letter from a client requesting a copy of something, you probably don't drop everything to rush off and take care of the request immediately. If a particular e-mail is going to take some research before responding, print it out and put it in your pending file until you have the time to devote to that task.

If you bill $200/hr and can regain even 15 minutes per day by eliminating certain timewasters, you can potentially add $8,650 to your bottom line. Doesn't that make giving up Free Cell just a tad bit easier?

> *Tip: Take a close look at how your personal habits are impacting your business. Maybe it's time to make a few changes.*

TIPS TO HELP YOU MANAGE YOUR TIME

- Use a planner to track appointments and tasks. It can be a paper-based notebook, a computer software program, or an electronic handheld device.

- Make a habit of prioritizing your weekly tasks. Rank them in order of importance.

- Review how you are spending your time and make adjustments according to your goals and priorities.

- Create at least one hour of uninterrupted time per day to tackle projects and action items.

- Allocate more time for a task than you think it will take to allow for interruptions.

- Break large projects down into small, sequential steps. Schedule these steps into your day with your planner.

- Group errands together so that you save time (and money) on travel, and the hassle of having to run out again because you didn't plan your trip initially.

- Work while you wait. Have busy work on hand to do while you wait at the doctor's office, are on hold with the cable company, or are stuck waiting for a late lunch date.

- Create time management goals. For example, set a goal that you will not take personal phone calls while you're working.

- Track your activities to determine whether or not you're accomplishing your time management goals.

- Establish routines and stick to them as much as possible.

- Be sure your systems are organized. If you waste a lot of time looking for files on your computer, take the time to organize a file management system.

[Provided by the National Association of Professional Organizers, www.napo@napo.net]

21

SUCCESS AFORETHOUGHT:
YOUR FIRM IN TEN YEARS

When you started your small firm practice, where did you expect to go with it? Are you there yet? In looking at your firm today, what parts of it had you originally envisioned, and what parts were not in your early vision?

My first job as a legal secretary was in a firm in San Francisco that was 101 years old when I arrived. I would love to have known what the founding fathers had envisioned when they joined together to form their new law firm. They could not possibly have imagined the Mag Tape Word Processor equipment that so amazed me with its ability to produce endless originals of a document simply by running the punched paper tape through a reader device time and time again.

They certainly never would have imagined that in 1971, in honor of the firm's 100th anniversary, the attorneys would be allowed to walk out of their private offices without their suit jackets on for the first time. (And, they certainly wouldn't have believed that this would be a non-issue for some of the attorneys because they were, dare I say it, women!)

They would have been stunned to know that in a couple more years, the firm would be one of the first in the city to have a fax machine, capable of transmitting documents over the phone lines at the dizzying rate of six minutes per page.

While in 1972, we didn't foresee the approach of cutting-edge technology in the form of the IBM Correcting Selectric, the firm's founders had never seen a typewriter, or even heard the word "typewriter." Computer? You're kidding, right?

Mr. Chickering and Mr. Gregory would have been mightily distrustful of the fancy flying machines that their 20th century employees were using to get from one side of the country to the other in service to their clients. The train was plenty good enough for getting to their out-of-town clients for at least two generations of attorneys. Indeed, the trip from the Bay Area to Southern California was a most enjoyable way to spend 18–24 hours, with frequent stops to pick up and set down passengers in many of California's rural communities. Travel time was a best guess, dependent on how many cows wandered onto the tracks along the way.

I doubt the senior gentlemen envisioned the firm growing to 35 attorneys, with the secretarial positions being occupied by women (many of them young and living on their own).

Move ahead to 1986, when I left my last law firm to start my own business. The firm had just ordered its first two desktop computers. The management committee allowed us to buy only two because they wanted to see if there was enough advantage to having this equipment to justify buying a few more. The firm administrator devised a plan to place one computer on each floor of the office so that multiple secretaries could share this new-fangled device on an as-needed basis.

One of the firm's attorneys was a beta tester for Kaypro. When he was done with his test period, he sold me his used Kaypro II ($1,200) for my new business. I thought New Word was the greatest thing I'd ever seen—not to mention Space Invaders, which I played by the hour.

iPhones? Say what? A Blackberry? A key ingredient in my favorite pie. E-mail? Isn't that the Cockney form of "He male?" Laptops? Okay, you've totally lost me now.

The point of all this is that ***whatever your original vision was/is for your practice, if it's more than five years old, it's out of date***. Five years from now, your current vision will be out of date, and so it goes. Technology is advancing at hyperspeed, your clients' needs are changing as the world they live in changes; staffing your firm no longer requires an employee to work side-by-side with you in a brick-and-mortar office; attorneys are now offering services they had never heard of five years ago; and a solo attorney in a town of 800 people can represent clients from around the world.

The only constant is change.

You are at a pivotal point. You're on the brink of your future. What an exciting place to be! What's more, you've got the ability to make it whatever you want it to be. Think about it. If your heart's desire is to have a virtual law firm employing attorneys and support staff all around the world, it can be yours. If your dreams run to building a practice around helping pro se parties prepare for and represent themselves in court, there's nothing to stop you. If you want to set up an immigration practice on the border and help immigrants come into this country legally, go for it. If you choose to have the first intergalactic law practice, you could do it! All right, maybe that last one's a stretch, but the point is that if you develop a vision for your practice, you can become that.

Think big, think expansively, and think possibilities. Set your sights on what you want to be, not what tradition says you should be. Let me warn you, though, this won't be an easy exercise for you. Attorneys tell me that law school smashes the heck out of students' natural creativity. The best ideas come from thinking outside the box, but attorneys are trained to work within the box. Let's face it, if it weren't for precedent, your job would be a lot tougher. You are taught to consider who else has done this, and how has it worked for them? Who else has argued this point and what did the court do with that? What case law can I find that will help my client?

I spend a lot of time thinking about my clients, their problems, and their goals. Luckily for my clients, I am blessed with an abundance of God-given creativity and original ideas. My friends and family get a kick out of the fact that it's just about impossible for me not to "consult" because the ideas just start flooding out of me. If someone presents me with a situation, I take it as a personal challenge and I just can't turn off the solutions tap.

My job is to come up with fresh ideas to help my clients gain a competitive edge, become more efficient, make more money, get the type and number of clients they want, and so forth. You achieve these goals not by copying what other law firms are doing, but *by doing things that no one else is doing*. That said, you can imagine my frustration when I present a thrilling new idea to my client only to hear, "Hmmm. Who else is doing this and how's it working for them?" This is the kiss of death and the attorney has completely missed the point.

So, for the sake of crafting your own vision, forget about what other firms are doing, unless you can take it a step further and do it better.

Where will you be in 10 years?

Now, let's switch gears for a minute and do a little time traveling (all you Dr. Who fans, think "TARDIS"). We're going to take a look at your firm's future.

Read these questions carefully, then sit back, close your eyes, put everything else out of your mind. Cut loose the imagination, and let the dreaming begin.

It's today's date, only 10 years from now. It's first thing in the morning, and you are sitting in your work environment, enjoying a few minutes of quiet reflection. Look around you. Get in touch with your surroundings.

- Where are you seated?
- Describe the room in detail. The colors on the walls? The style of décor? The artwork? Your personal mementos? The windows? The sounds?
- Are you alone? If not, who is with you?
- How are you feeling?

- What are you going to do today?
- Where will you do it?
- How do you feel about the task(s) or activity(ies) ahead of you?
- Who will help you with your work?
- How many employees do you have working with you?
- Who will you be doing this for?
- Who are your clients? Describe them in detail.
- How much money will the firm gross this year?
- How much money will you make personally?
- What tools help you with efficiency and productivity?
- How would you describe your technology?
- How many hours do you plan to work today?
- What billing method are you using?
- What is your main practice area? Additional practice areas?
- What services are you providing to your clients?
- Describe your level of satisfaction with your practice.
- How do you feel about where you are in your career?
- Who is waiting for you at home?
- Are you happy?

Welcome to your vision! Start planning and taking steps today to make your vision a reality. If you aren't crazy about this vision, don't worry, you have 10 years to develop a better future than the one you just imagined!

The future is only a minute away, so there's no time to lose. Get clear on your vision and get moving. You can either take control of your future, or be a victim of it. The choice is yours.

> *Tip: The future will come whether or not you are ready.*
> *Meet it head on with a vision for success!*

22

MY GOALS:
AN ACTION PLAN FOR SUCCESS

Repeat after me: This year is going to be *my* year! I know where I want to go and how I'm going to get there. I'm choosing three goals for my practice this year that will help take it to a new level and give me even more satisfaction! I know that the most successful goals are SMART goals:

S	=	Specific (e.g., lower my overhead, improve collections)
M	=	Measurable (e.g., 45 percent overhead, 90 percent (or more) realization rate, five new referral sources)
A	=	Achievable (is this actually possible?)
R	=	Realistic (do I have the necessary training, resources, tools, staff, time?)
T	=	Timed (what's my deadline or timeframe?)

I'm going to concentrate on the three significant goals stated here as SMART goals, along with an action plan to achieve each:

GOAL #1

S = _____

_____

M = _____

_____

A = _____

_____

R = _____

_____

T = _____

_____

The steps I need to take to reach this goal are (list as many steps as you need):

1. _____

_____

2. _____

_____

3. _____

_____

4. _____

_____

5. _____

_____

GOAL #2

S = _____

_____

M = _____

_____

A = _____

_____

R = _____

_____

T   = _____

_____

The steps I need to take to reach this goal are (list as many steps as you need):

1.   _____

_____

2.   _____

_____

3.   _____

_____

4.   _____

_____

5.   _____

_____

GOAL #3

S   = _____

_____

M   = _____

_____

A   = _____

_____

R   = _____

_____

T   = _____

_____

The steps I need to take to reach this goal are (list as many steps as you need):

1. _____
   _____

2. _____
   _____

3. _____
   _____

4. _____
   _____

5. _____
   _____

This is going to take some work on my part, but it will be worth it. Achieving my goals will allow me to: _____

_____
_____
_____

As a reward for my hard work, I will treat myself with: _____

_____
_____
_____

Stand back, world, because I mean business! I'm breaking out and moving up! I'm becoming the attorney I was meant to be with the practice I was meant to have!!

Date _____ _____

Your Signature

23

IN A NUTSHELL:
25 WAYS TO INCREASE PROFITABILITY
WITHOUT WORKING HARDER

Dorothy, a solo practitioner, is constantly struggling financially. Her yearend numbers for last year were disappointing, yet she is working long hours and can't see any way to work more to increase her revenues. Can she make more money and meet her financial goals? You bet—and it won't require her to work any harder. In fact, she just might be able to cut back on her hours a bit if she'll make a few changes in the way she manages her time and her practice.

Applying the lessons found elsewhere in this book, let's look at how Dorothy can boost her revenues with proactive management strategies, and make this her best year ever. While each action has a potential impact on the bottom line, some directly affect, and others indirectly affect, profitability. If Dorothy adopts even a few of these strategies, she'll see a positive difference in her practice – and a definite increase in her revenues.

1. ***Have a plan.*** Dorothy needs a business plan to help guide her business decisions. Making important choices only after consulting the business plan will help Dorothy avoid making impulsive decisions that can waste time and money and take her away from her goals for the practice.

   POTENTIAL IMPACT: Not measurable

2. ***Get her fees right.*** If Dorothy isn't making enough money, her billing rate might not be sufficient to meet her financial needs. She needs to revisit her current fees to determine if they are right for her. As an example, let's say that Dorothy bills and collects on 1,200 hours per year. If she raises her $200 rate by 10 percent to $220, she will increase her annual billings by $24,000.

   POTENTIAL IMPACT: $24,000/yr

3. *Make technology her friend.* If Dorothy becomes more familiar with her current software, she will probably discover a number of timesaving features that will help her increase her efficiency and productivity. As an example, a good document assembly program can cut a six-hour job down to 20 minutes. Using templates, auto features, and macros in her word processing program can also save a few minutes here and there. With a PDA, Dorothy can handle billable tasks away from the office. Instead of wandering the halls of the courthouse waiting for a hearing to begin, Dorothy can check her e-mail, communicate with clients, update her calendar, phone opposing counsel, and so forth. More potential billable time. For figures' sake, let's say that Dorothy's PDA allows her to bill 15 minutes more per day. At $200/hr, those fees add up quickly.

   POTENTIAL IMPACT: $8,650/yr

4. *Get organized.* An organized office is a tremendous boon to productivity. If Dorothy organizes her office for maximum efficiency, she will regain billable time previously spent searching for things. Look what happens if she can regain and bill an additional 15 hours per year through a more organized work environment.

   POTENTIAL IMPACT: $3,000/yr

5. *Delegate.* If Dorothy can regain even three hours per month by delegating tasks that are not the best use of her time, she can put that time to better use working on billable matters. These tasks might include bookkeeping, filing, website updates, drafting routine documents and letters, newsletter preparation, and so on.

   POTENTIAL IMPACT: $7,200/yr

6. *Watch her numbers.* Regularly reviewing financial statements will help Dorothy monitor her revenues and expenses, and allow her to compare her actual expenses to her projected budget for the year. She can save herself time and headaches, as well as increase her revenues, by closely monitoring, and adjusting for, the financial position of her practice.

   POTENTIAL IMPACT: Not measurable

7. *Improve her realization rate.* Dorothy's current realization rate is 84 percent on average billings of $20,000 per month. If Dorothy can bring her rate up to 90 percent, she will be pleased with the increase in her revenues.

   POTENTIAL IMPACT: $14,400/yr

8. *Evergreen deposit account.* Using a replenishing advance fee deposit will help Dorothy get paid timely and in full. The key here is that she must take an adequate deposit up front to insure that she will be able to pay herself if the client doesn't pay a monthly statement.

   POTENTIAL IMPACT: Not measurable

9. ***Bill promptly, accurately, and in detail.*** Dorothy should send out client bills on a regular basis, and her bills should clearly state what she did on behalf of her client, and the value of those services to her client. She'll find that her clients are much more likely to pay her bills if they understand the benefit they receive from her work.

POTENTIAL IMPACT: Not measurable

10. ***Attack accounts receivable early on.*** Dorothy needs to start her collections procedure as soon as an account becomes past due. The faster she moves, the higher her potential recovery can be. Dorothy's written fee agreement will give her guidance on determining when an account is past due.

POTENTIAL IMPACT: Not measurable

11. ***Contemporaneous timekeeping.*** If Dorothy captures even an additional one-tenth of an hour (six minutes) per day, she will see a noticeable difference in her year-end revenues.

POTENTIAL IMPACT: $4,796/yr

12. ***Hone her case and client selection skills.*** Like most attorneys, Dorothy has had a client or two with whom she would never want to work again. Bad clients sap an attorney's time, energy, and resources, and frequently end up not paying the attorney's bill. As Dorothy gains experience in assessing potential clients and their legal issues, she will develop the sensors that will warn her off certain clients.

POTENTIAL IMPACT: Not measurable

13. ***Limit pro bono work.*** Dorothy generously volunteers her time and skills to legal clinics and to clients without the financial means to secure legal representation on their own. This is terrific, but she needs to plan her pro bono time so that it doesn't significantly impact her practice. Four or five hours of pro bono work per month, on average, is usually a reasonable and manageable amount for a solo or small firm attorney. Too much pro bono work can hurt her practice and then she won't be able to help her worthy causes.

POTENTIAL IMPACT: Not measurable

14. ***Set billable or revenue goals.*** Dorothy's low revenues may be due, in part, to three things: (1) she doesn't know her breakeven point; (2) she doesn't know her realization rate, so she isn't clear on how much she needs to bill each week to cover her expenses and compensation; or (3) the goals that worked last year may be too low to cover her needs now. If Dorothy sets a goal based on her needs, and monitors her progress in achieving that goal each month, her low-revenues problem may just go away.

POTENTIAL IMPACT: Not measurable

15. *Focus her practice.* A specialized, or focused, practice earns, on average, 10-15 percent more than a general practice. Dorothy may not have developed a focus and an expertise that would boost her productivity or allow her to charge what she needs to meet her goals.

    POTENTIAL IMPACT: Not measurable

16. *Market, market, market.* If Dorothy isn't making enough money, she may not have enough work, or she may not be working with the right clients for her practice. Dorothy may need to spend more time on marketing activities to help her fill the pipeline, attract her ideal clients, and increase her revenues.

    POTENTIAL IMPACT: Not measurable

17. *Charge for initial consultations.* While some practices traditionally don't charge for initial consultations, Dorothy's real estate practice can and should. Some attorneys charge a flat fee and limit the time they will spend in an initial consultation. Others charge their regular hourly rate for that first meeting. If Dorothy charges $100 for an initial consultation, and she averages four consultations per month, she will add $400 per month to her revenues.

    POTENTIAL IMPACT: $4,800/yr

18. *Eliminate timewasters.* Dorothy conducted an assessment of how she spends her work time, and made some startling discoveries about how certain common (and previously unrecognized) habits are cutting into her potential billable time. Eliminating timewasters can have a nice impact on her potential revenues.

ACTION TAKEN	DAILY GAIN
• Deleted games folder from computer	15 mins.
• Reads newspapers at home, rather than in the office	30 mins.
• Stopped reading personal e-mail from family and friends during work hours	20 mins.
• Stopped reading the headline news on her ISP's home page during the business day	10 mins.
• Stopped aimlessly surfing the internet in search of travel bargains, recipes, former classmates, gardening tips, and size AAA width shoes for her daughter, etc.	20 mins.
TOTAL TIME GAINED	95 mins.

    POTENTIAL IMPACT: $54,984/yr

19. *Bill 15 minutes more each day.* Dorothy found that if she made better use of her time, she could actually bill 15 minutes more per day without any trouble. When she had a few minutes to spare (waiting for a lunch date to arrive, waiting for a

return call, or approaching quitting time), Dorothy purposefully picked up another billable task. Even if she knew that she would not be able to complete the task that day, she at least got it started. After all, she would have to work those 15 minutes on the project at some point. Why not do it today and get that time recorded on her timesheet.

POTENTIAL IMPACT: $8,650/yr

20. *Listen to her staff.* Staff and attorneys sometimes look at things from different perspectives. Staff is frequently more aware of inefficiencies and blocks to productivity than are attorneys. Dorothy can save time and money by soliciting her assistant's insight on how the office is operating and what could make it more efficient.

POTENTIAL IMPACT: Not measurable

21. *Get plenty of rest.* The negative impact of sleep-deprivation has been thoroughly documented in recent years. Dorothy must take care of her physical self to be her best professional self. A full night's sleep, periodic vacations, relaxed weekends, regular exercise, healthy diet—all contribute to a balanced lifestyle, increased energy, increased ability to focus on the tasks at hand, clarity of mind, and so forth. All can impact the bottom line.

POTENTIAL IMPACT: Not measurable

22. *Respect her clients.* Invaluable advice. Dorothy needs to treat her clients well and make them feel as important to her as they are. Satisfied clients are more likely to pay your statements promptly and give you referrals, and are less likely to file a bar complaint or a malpractice suit. The added bonus is that treating your clients with respect can just make the working relationship a whole lot more pleasant.

POTENTIAL IIMPACT: Not measurable

23. *Add value to her services.* To stand out from the competition, Dorothy needs to add value to her current services. She needs to think about what she can do to meet her clients' needs—what she can offer that other attorneys are not providing. She'll have happier clients (who are delighted to make referrals) and attract more clients when she gets known for exceeding her clients' expectations.

POTENTIAL IMPACT: Not measurable

24. *Set business goals.* To improve her practice, Dorothy would do well to set new challenges for herself each year. She can zero in on one or two specific goals she wants to achieve, and then develop the plan that will help her do that. As an example, Dorothy may want to spend more time marketing this year. She may want to create additional visibility for herself and her practice, or she may choose

to hire an associate attorney. The key to this is setting realistic and achievable goals. Knowing where you are going helps you get there.

POTENTIAL IMPACT: Not measurable

25. ***Become proactive as a manager.*** For too many years, Dorothy has let her practice be directed by circumstances or events, rather than by a plan. She has operated in default mode, reacting to problems and situations instead of planning for success. Managing a practice only when absolutely necessary is not conducive to success. Reactive managers tend to wait until they are forced to manage. Proactive managers watch for business opportunities and pursue them, when appropriate, as well as take steps to head off future problems. They regularly take action to guide and nurture their businesses and usually enjoy a higher level of success and satisfaction with their practices.

POTENTIAL IMPACT: Not measurable

Dorothy has a lot of tips to choose from if she wants to increase her profitability and eliminate some of her money worries. If Dorothy took all of the actions listed above and achieved the same quantifiable results, she could add more than ***$130,480*** this year to her bottom line—and all without working harder. If she's generating revenues sufficient to cover her expenses and provide her with the level of compensation she wants, she's bound to feel more satisfaction with a practice that is supporting her.

What can you do to increase profitability without working harder?

> *Tip: Making more money isn't always about working*
> *harder—often it's simply a matter of working smarter!*

24

THE FIVE Rs:
HOW TO KEEP YOUR STAFF WITH YOU FOREVER

As a law firm manager in the '80s, one of my responsibilities was hiring legal secretaries for a mid-sized firm in Los Angeles. When I started with the firm, we had 38 legal secretaries. By the time I left, the firm had grown to employ 65 secretaries. At times, it seemed as though I did nothing other than interview and review résumés all day long. Nevertheless, I had the easy part: recruiting good staff. The attorneys had the hard part: retaining good staff.

The firm's turnover was really quite low for a 135-attorney firm; however, there were a few desks that came open several times a year. The challenge was to find secretaries who not only had good skills, but who were also blessed with hides like rhinos. Not an easy task then, and nearly impossible now when there is such a shortage of skilled support staff.

Employee turnover doesn't show up on any of your firm's financial statements, but it certainly impacts profitability. It costs upwards of $25,000 to replace a legal assistant. Not many small firms can handle an expense like that without feeling some pain.

To be a successful manager, you must take care of your staff. The return on investment will be immeasurable. Your office will be a more supportive, productive, and pleasant place to work and your clients will be well cared for when you have good and happy staff.

Sometimes you cause employees to leave.

Much of the responsibility for the exodus of good employees lies with the attorneys themselves.

Here's a news flash: If you treat people well, most will respond in kind. If you don't, they leave. A simple concept, but not everyone gets it. An attorney in my former firm once told me that, "Staff are like paper towels—you use them up and throw them away." (Did I mention that this fellow went through 16 secretaries in the year before he joined our firm?)

As we take a look at the personal stories of four legal secretaries, you should be able to readily separate the winning bosses from the losing bosses. It won't be hard to predict the outcome in each situation. We'll start with Danielle.

Bad behavior makes you look foolish and costs you both in turnover and reputation.

Danielle could hardly wait to tell her friends that she had landed a plum job as personal assistant to the Executive Vice President/General Counsel of a major studio in Hollywood. Danielle was highly intelligent, organized, efficient, and her technical skills were far above average. This seemed the perfect job for her.

Danielle was cool and calm in any situation, but her serene demeanor was put to the test during her second week on the job. Her boss called her to bring files to him at his home. When Danielle rang the doorbell, her new boss answered the door stark naked. He invited her in, led her to his office, took a seat, and proceeded to dictate several letters. Finally, the VP couldn't stand it any longer and asked if she wasn't going to say anything about his appearance. He seemed disappointed that Danielle had shown no visible reaction to his astonishing display–after all, she'd gotten a mighty good view at the door. When Danielle replied that she "didn't see anything to get excited about," he blew up and ordered her from the house. The following week, he tried the same thing with another new assistant in his office. Turns out, this was a little performance he liked to give for the benefit of all new hires.

After enduring harassment and verbal abuse from this man for six months, the final straw for Danielle came out of the blue one day. The VP ordered lunch to be served in his office. When Danielle delivered his meal, the VP took exception to the food, picked up a plate of spaghetti and hurled it at her. She ducked and the tomato sauce and pasta hit the wall. He was furious and began spewing expletives and calling Danielle names she'd never even heard before. The source of his rage? Danielle. The guy was furious that she had dodged the plate, thereby allowing the food to ruin his grass cloth wallcovering.

Danielle returned to her desk, typed out her resignation, handed it to a coworker, and walked out the door. (As a reminder, that reprehensible, infantile, and actionable behavior came out of a licensed practitioner of law.)

Disregarding your employees' feelings and needs is a form of victimization and it will come back to bite you in the end.

The next story is that of Nikki, secretary to a solo real estate attorney. For three years, Nikki toiled away at her job, juggling reception duties with paralegal drafting and research projects, preparing client bills, and handling all secretarial duties. For three years, her attorney told her that he valued her work, but that there simply wasn't enough money in the coffers to allow him to give her a raise in salary, or much in the way of any benefits. "But when things pick up, I'll take care of you" always brought an end to any discussion of money.

So, Nikki struggled on, bringing her lunch every day, riding the bus to work to hold down her expenses, shopping at discount stores, and believing that her boss would take care of her when things got better.

One fine day, Nikki was working at her desk when her attorney came bounding into the office, flushed of face and in an obvious state of elation. "Nikki, come down to the parking lot. I've got to show you something. You're not going to believe your eyes!" Truer words were never spoken.

In the parking lot, the attorney brought Nikki face to face with her long-promised raise—in the form of the attorney's brand-new dark blue Mercedes 450 SLE.

"Isn't she a beauty?" he crowed. "All my life I've dreamed of having a Mercedes, and now it's mine. I deserve it. I've arrived! Of course, we're going to have to cut some corners so I can pay for it, but you're great at finding ways to save money, so I know we can do it."

After murmuring a few words of faint praise for the sleek automobile, Nikki went back upstairs, got out the employment ads in the local legal newspaper, and began making calls to set up interviews for a new job. Within a week, Nikki had a job offer with a 40 percent increase in pay and full benefits. Nikki left with two days' notice and no regrets—other than having stayed loyal for three years to someone who obviously didn't care a thing about her.

Sometimes you cause employees to stay.

The responsibility for developing and keeping good employees rests squarely on your shoulders.

Story number three involves Amy. She was hired by a firm to work for a partner considered to be impossible. Fortunately, Amy didn't know this or she might have been frightened off. Amy's willingness to learn fostered a level of patience in the attorney that few had seen up to this point. He expected the work to be done timely and correctly, and

Amy didn't let him down. Over time, the attorney developed a high level of trust in Amy's intelligence and her ability to handle any task assigned her. He gave her more and more responsibility, and she always rose to the occasion. Eventually, he had Amy sit in on public utility commission hearings in which the firm's largest client had an interest, but was not a party. She would transcribe her notes into a memo to her attorney, and he would forward the memo under Amy's name to the vice president of the client company. The firm's associate attorneys were instructed to have "The Boss" (as her boss had come to call Amy) review all documents prepared for the partner's signature before he would sign them. Eventually, she began to draft routine documents for filing with the state public utilities commission and the FPC.

Amy's attorney was not prone to effusive praise, but he always said thank you for work done, and he clearly demonstrated in so many ways that he relied on her and trusted her. As she told him years later, "You always treated me as though I could do anything," to which he replied, "Well, you could and you can."

At one point, Amy's car died and she couldn't afford to repair it. For the first time in her life, she had to rely on public transportation to get anywhere. Living in a suburb of the city, transportation back and forth to work was available, but there was virtually no way for her to get around her residential community other than on foot.

During this time, the attorney took a month-long vacation to Europe and asked Amy to "look after my car—and drive it as much as possible to keep the battery charged." When he returned from the trip, he asked Amy if she would be willing to work for him on some personal projects in the evenings and on weekends to help him with some family business. He would, of course, pay her out of his own pocket, at a rate significantly higher than her daytime rate. Amy gratefully agreed, and found to her amazement, that the work lasted exactly as long as it took her to save up enough money to buy her neighbor's used car.

Eventually, the attorney had a great opportunity to go in-house with a new start-up company; the bad news was that he would be sharing a secretary with the vice president and she was already there. No place for Amy. Never mind, because Amy quickly found a job working in the legal department of an airline. It was a union job and she had to take a 25 percent cut in pay; still, the travel benefits were unbelievable and the sweet smell of adventure overrode the need to make money.

After several months, Amy and the attorney ran into each other, and she told him all about her new job and the travel opportunities. He asked where she had flown to first, and she admitted that she had been unable to travel because of the big pay cut. "But, one day . . . ."

Oddly, it turned out that their meeting was fortuitous because the attorney needed more after-hours help with his family business. The extra money Amy earned from the moonlighting put her income slightly above where she had been before she joined the airline, and she was able to fly her mother to Mazatlán for a long weekend to celebrate her birthday that year.

Some 37 years later, Amy and the attorney are still friends. Amy would do anything in the world for this fellow that others in their old law firm had written off as being cold, formal, and difficult. Amy saw none of that in him. All she knew was how he treated her and she never found another boss who came anywhere near the level of respect and responsibility that this lawyer bestowed on her. The attorney has long since retired from the practice of law, but Amy has often remarked that had his new company offered her a job too, she would have stayed with him forever.

Sometimes something as simple as a sincere thank you is enough.

Our last story involves Linda, a secretary in her firm's secretarial pool. Declared legally blind, Linda was conscious of her limitations, and bent over backwards to make up for her inability to handle copy typing by volunteering for all the tasks the other secretaries didn't want to do. Consequently, Linda spent her days happily transcribing tapes, Bates stamping documents, and tabbing and organizing exhibits. She more than earned her keep by cheerfully tackling the jobs that others detested.

Late one afternoon, the office manager was asked to find someone to stay and help with some last minute photocopying for a trial the next day. She was warned that it could be a very late night. Her first thought was Linda. She knew that Linda would jump at the chance to be helpful, and, besides, no one else would ever volunteer for overtime that involved hours of photocopying.

As expected, Linda was thrilled to be asked to help out with such an important task, and was humming away at one of the copy machines when the office manager left at about 6:00 p.m.

When the office manager arrived at work around 8:30 a.m. the next morning, there was Linda standing at the copy machine—in the same dress she was wearing the day before, and looking decidedly blurry-eyed. She was just finishing up, she explained. Two of the copiers had broken down during the night, and she had been hard-pressed to complete the project in time for the attorney to race off to court.

Just then, the attorney came around the corner and told Linda, "Go home and get some sleep—you've certainly earned it." Linda demurred, but finally agreed to be sent home in a taxi at firm expense. That afternoon, an enormous arrangement of flowers was delivered to Linda's home with a simple note that said, "Thank you. I couldn't have managed without you!" and signed with the attorney's name.

Linda is still with the firm, some 29 years later. She's the first to volunteer when the attorney from the all-nighter needs overtime help. She would do anything for him, and he always expresses his appreciation to her, usually with just a heartfelt thank you. Often, that's all that's required.

There are thousands of such stories about both good attorney bosses and bad ones, and good firms and bad firms. The stories I shared here seem to be no-brainers—it's easy to see why secretaries left or stayed. But not all ill treatment is so easily identified.

The 5 Rs that will keep your staff with you forever.

Starting with my tenure as a law firm manager, I've asked thousands of law firm employees to name the one thing they want most from attorneys. Can you guess the resounding answer?

Think Aretha Franklin.

R-E-S-P-E-C-T.

Are you surprised that money wasn't the leading answer? You shouldn't be. We all operate with the same basic needs. Being treated with respect is way up the list of what motivates, validates, fulfills, and improves self-esteem for us.

So, how do you keep your staff happy? The same way you keep your clients happy— by meeting their needs. I've distilled the five leading answers I've received from support staff over the years into what I call "The Five Rs That Will Keep Your Staff With You Forever." [DISCLAIMER: Oh, yeah, about that "keeping them forever" part, results may vary in your firm.]

Pretty much in this order, your staff wants:

1. *Respect*

   As the lead litigation secretary in my former firm once told me, "I want these attorneys to understand that I am a legal secretary because I want to be. This is my career choice. It's not because I'm too stupid for law school; it's because this is what I've always wanted to do. I belong to a professional association of law firm support staff. I'm constantly taking classes to upgrade my skills. I take pride in my work and the supportive role I play for my attorney. I'm living my dream." A J.D. doesn't make one person better than another and it certainly doesn't make one person smarter than another (as demonstrated in the stories above). As children, we all learned the basics of respect, beginning with the magic words, "please" and "thank you." Apply liberally with your staff and enjoy the reward!

2. *Responsibility*

   Remember Amy? Most people get tired of doing the same old thing over and over, and your support staff is no exception. Shake things up once in awhile. Let them tackle new tasks. Give them permission to make mistakes while they are learning new procedures. Help them develop new skills by providing additional training. You'll only be the better for helping someone else reach his or her potential.

3. *Recognition*

Your employees want to be recognized for the contribution they make to your firm. Tell your employees frequently how much you value them—and brag about them to others, in front of your employees. One solo practitioner is in the habit of creating treats for his secretary of many years. One day he noticed an art show going on in the plaza next to his office building, so he took his secretary out to view the display, then insisted they get an ice cream cone before returning to work. Who wouldn't want to work with a guy like that! During the summer months, everyone in one small firm votes for the "Employee of the Week." This employee is selected for attitude, helpfulness, kindness, professionalism, and contribution to the firm. At the morning coffee break on Friday, the winner is announced for the week. That person gets to leave at noon for the rest of the day (full pay for the afternoon, of course). You don't have to spend a lot of money, but you do have to be sincere. Lip service doesn't cut it. Your actions will always make a stronger statement about the importance of your staff to you than will your words.

4. *Remembrance*

This is different from recognition. It's about remembering who is on your team and who has your back. As an example, I can't even count the number of times I've seen this sort of thing happen. A trial is due to start in a week. Attorneys and staff alike are burning the midnight oil in preparation for the big day. Finally, the trial begins, and the outcome is in favor of the firm's client. The attorneys return triumphantly from court, high fiving each other in the hallway, and boasting about how great they were. Finally, they decide to take the celebration across the street to their favorite watering hole, so out the door the rollicking group scoots. And, who's left behind? The paralegal who missed her brother's wedding because of the massive trial preparation required. The single mother who drove two hours across Los Angeles in commute traffic to pick up her kids from daycare and take them to her mother's home for the night, then drove two hours back to the office to work, day after day. The office services manager who took two buses across town in the middle of the night when the high-speed copier broke down in the middle of copying exhibits. These wonderful folks are called *support* staff for a reason. Remember your employees for making all things possible for you.

5. *Remuneration*

Lastly, your employees want to be paid fairly. It's interesting, but I'm more likely to find staff clamoring for top dollar when they aren't getting enough of the other

Rs. If they are treated with respect, given additional responsibility commensurate with their abilities, recognized and remembered, money isn't such a big issue. Too many employers believe that throwing more money at staff will keep them happy. That is simply not the case. Still, you must treat them fairly. Do the best you can for them with salary and benefits. They deserve it.

Several years ago, I had a conversation with Michael Coe, then Vice President of Seattle's highly successful Gene Juarez Salons & Spas chain. I asked Mr. Coe the secret of his company's success, and his answer may surprise you.

Mr. Coe admitted candidly that his business was not always so successful. He said that for many years, the company's priorities were inverted: (1) clients; (2) company; and (3) employees. About 10 years previous to our conversation, he realized that this was wrong thinking. A trip to the beauty salon is meant to be a relaxing and rejuvenating experience; however, if the salon employees weren't happy, their dissatisfaction would seep through into their interactions with the clients, and his salons would lose clients for more upbeat and happier environments. Mr. Coe said, "It's not that we mistreated our employees. We just thought of them as a means to an end."

So, the company made a conscious shift in focus: keeping employees happy, challenged, well paid, and supported was now the company's top priority. Mr. Coe said that this change in thinking has led to the company's current level of success. Because the company has been putting its emphasis on the employees, productivity has increased many times over. Their employees look for ways to better serve their clients. The client count has grown by leaps and bounds. Clients look forward to a visit to the salon, and they are eager to refer their friends. In turn, the company's revenues have far exceeded the owners' wildest expectations.

Pay attention to the lessons learned by this business owner. No matter how well you are doing in this area, there is still room for improvement.

[P.S. I know from personal experience what it takes to keep your staff happy. You see, in the story above, Amy is not the secretary's real name. It's Ann, and the story is mine.]

> *Tip: If you experience high turnover, chances are you need to be doing something differently.*

25

ANNUAL RETREAT:
THE YEAR BEHIND, THE YEAR AHEAD

There's a reason that large firms hold annual retreats and small firms don't. Large firms generally have a plan, or business strategy, and small firms don't. Larger firms use an annual retreat as a time to get away from the office and its distractions to focus on strategic planning for the next year and beyond. Small firms frequently are focused on the end of the month, and not much beyond that.

The reality is that it doesn't matter the size of your firm. An annual retreat is a valuable management tool that affords you the opportunity to take stock of where you've come from, and develop a plan for where you're going. It's important to spend some quality time examining past successes and failures, and crafting a strategy for moving the firm forward. It's a healthy thing to do for your practice, and you need to do it. You need to take time away from everything and just think about business for a day or two. As Martha Stewart would say, "An annual retreat is a good thing."

Okay, so how do you handle your retreat? Enquiring minds want to know.

Where should I hold my retreat?

Selecting an appropriate location for your retreat is the first step. It's difficult to focus on your business when you are in your regular work environment. It's virtually impossible to ignore a client phone call, the mail, and your e-mail inbox when you are in your own office. By the same token, trying to hold your retreat in your home is equally unsatisfactory because kids, pets, spouses, phones, and mail don't get that you aren't to be interrupted for anything.

Large law firms hold annual retreats at posh resorts, where there are few distractions (except for the siren call of the golf course), to allow the firm's attorneys to focus on the business, away from the business.

As a solo or small firm practitioner, you also need a respite from the pressures of juggling a law practice with management responsibilities. You need to put some time into thinking about where you want your practice to go, and how you're going to get there. Book yourself into a nice hotel, inn, or B&B that is at least 50 miles from home for three nights. [NOTE: The reason for the 50-mile minimum is to get you out of your everyday environment and open you up to new scenery, new experiences, new food, and new ideas. Trust me, you aren't going to get the same benefit out of your retreat if you're staying at the Travelodge in the heart of your hometown.] Some basic considerations in choosing your location are:

- quiet (e.g., not poolside in warm weather);
- peaceful;
- outside area for thoughtful walks;
- comfortable (enough space to feel relaxed);
- work space (desk or dinette table); and
- room service (optional for you maybe, not for me!).

Your packing list should include:

- comfortable clothes;
- your firm's financial statements (yearend profit and loss statements for the last three years, current aged accounts report, productivity reports by timekeeper, current balance sheet, etc.);
- your firm's business plan;
- your firm's marketing plan and your client tracking log (record of where your new clients come from);
- your firm's budget for last year and the coming year;
- a calculator, pens, and pads of paper.

Who should attend the retreat?

Please note that your packing list does not include family, dog, spouse, significant other, or mother-in-law. Family members or friends are lovely distractions, but the point of a retreat is to do some serious work on your business. So keep it just business—attorneys only.

All firm partners should attend. In many cases, there are none, so a solo retreat it will be. Consider inviting associate attorneys to join in the marketing and long-range planning sessions.

Check in on Thursday afternoon or evening and enjoy a nice dinner with some decompression time before turning in. Get a good night's sleep because you've got some heavy work to do tomorrow.

What should I do on my retreat?

Now that you're here, just what is it you are expected to do on this retreat? It's pretty simple, really. You're going to go over your business with a fine-toothed comb.

There are actually two phases to your retreat: (1) a review of the past year; and (2) planning for the coming year.

Day 1

Rise and shine. Switch off your cell phone. Have a good breakfast, and hit it!

You'll begin with a review of the previous year in terms of:

- The firm's financial situation (based on your various financial statements). Review your ratios and perform your calculations until you are satisfied that you understand your firm's financial strengths and weaknesses.

- A comparison of your yearend profit and loss statement with the budget for last year. Review these documents side-by-side, line-by line. See any disparities? Make notes, ask questions. Insure that you understand each category and the expenses allocated therein.

- Timekeeper productivity. Check billable hours and/or revenues generated. Compare to the cost of supporting each person. Are the timekeepers hitting their goals? If not, why not? What can you do to help them achieve their goals this year?

- Your overall marketing strategies. Review your tracking log to determine the effectiveness of your current plan and which strategies you may want to ramp up, change, or drop.

- The marketing efforts/effectiveness of each attorney (including yourself).

- Your firm's resources and how they were used.

- Use of staff.

- The overall effectiveness and contribution to the firm of each employee (including yourself).

- Your client satisfaction level.

You need to ask yourself some tough questions. Make notes, write out your answers, record your thoughts because you're going to want to refer back to them at the next retreat to see how things changed this year:

- What were your goals for last year? Which did you accomplish?
- Why were some not met?
- Did firm revenues meet your expectations? If not, why?
- Did your expenses work out to be as expected? If not, why?
- What was the average realization rate for each timekeeper last year?
- What didn't happen that you expected would happen?
- What happened that you didn't expect?
- Were your clients the people with whom you wanted to work? Why? Why not?
- What was your firm's overall marketing plan for the year?
- What did you do personally to market your firm? What did others do?
- How much time and money did you put into marketing?
- Did you get enough of the right clients/work? Why? Why not?
- What was your best source of new clients?
- What other services did you discover that your clients need or want?
- What did you do to make yourself more valuable to your clients last year?
- What was your best business decision last year? Why?
- What was your worst? Why?
- What were your firm's biggest successes last year? Why?
- Failures? Why?
- What are you proudest of with regard to last year?
- What do you hope no one will ask you about last year?
- What lessons did you learn from last year?
- What do you want to be able to report next year at this time?

This ought to keep you busy for most of the day. Be sure to take a few breaks during the day. You probably aren't used to thinking about the business with this intensity, or for this length of time, and I don't want you to hurt yourself! Go for a walk, go out for lunch, take a short nap, head to the lobby for a cup of coffee. Refresh yourself during the day because you have miles to go before you sleep.

When you've done all your work, call it a day. Treat yourself to a lovely meal, then get to bed early because, in the immortal words of Scarlett O'Hara, "Tomorrow is another day," and it's going to be equally busy.

Where do I go from here?

At this point, you are halfway through your retreat. You've done a good review of the past, identified the lessons learned, and are now ready to look ahead.

Day 2

Good morning! Today is all about tomorrow, and the day after that, and the day after that, and on into the future. Yesterday's work was all about where you've been. Today's work is all about where you're going. Work your way through these questions slowly and with great thought.

- Do you have any current issues that need to be resolved? What are some possible solutions? What steps will you take to resolve these issues?
- Who do you want to become?
- What do you personally want to be known for?
- What do you want your firm to become?
- What would that look like?
- What do you want your firm to be known for?
- What other service businesses have favorably impressed you recently? Why?
- How can you bring some of that into your firm?
- What new services can you add this year?
- What additional income streams can you develop?
- What is your budget for the coming year?
- Do you anticipate any capital expenditures this year? If so, how much and for what?
- Are these expenses necessary? Why? Why not?
- Where are you in your business plan right now?
- What must you do this next year to move your business plan forward?
- What will this look like? When will it happen? Who will be responsible?
- What marketing strategies will you choose for the coming year?
- What is your marketing budget for this year? What is included in that budget?

- Who will have primary responsibility for implementing your marketing strategies?

- What is the marketing role of each person in your firm?

- Do you have enough attorneys to handle the work? Enough staff? Who might you need to hire? Why is this person necessary? What tasks would this person handle? What would be the cost (including wage and benefits package)? Can you afford it? When would that happen? How will you recruit this person?

- What is the image you want your firm to project? How are you doing with that now? What do you plan to do during the coming year to improve or promote that image?

- What do you want to do better for your clients this next year? How will you do that?

- What are your goals for the year? (Include any billable goals, revenue goals, marketing goals, growth plans, etc.)

- What are your action steps to reach these goals?

- Who will be responsible for all or parts of these action steps?

- Where do you want to be one year from now vis-à-vis your business? Do you believe your current plan will get you there? Why? If not, what do you need to do differently to achieve your goals for the year?

Take good notes. Make lists. Write down all of your ideas (both the good and the not-so-good ones—no critiquing as you go). Dare to think outside the box! Don't think about what everyone else is doing, think of what you'd like to do.

Forget precedent for the day! Successful businesses are successful because they have developed a competitive advantage. They are the originators of new thinking and cutting-edge ideas, not followers of someone else's ideas. You can't get ahead by staying in the middle of the pack. If you want to stand out from other law firms, then you have to do something outstanding. Stop thinking of what is and start thinking about what could be!

Before you head for home, make sure you've developed an action plan to help you reach your goals. Prioritize the things you want to achieve this year and lay out the steps you'll take to accomplish those goals. Determine who will be responsible for the various steps and establish timelines for the work.

If your last year didn't turn out quite the way you had hoped, then repeating what you did last year won't get you where you want to go. If your year turned out better than you had expected, you'll still need to step up your game to reach an even higher level of success. Remember, if you keep doing what you've been doing, you'll keep getting what you've been getting.

Spending a few days working on your business and developing your action plan will pay off in the long run. A plan allows you to take charge of your future. A retreat allows you to return to the office refreshed and reinvigorated, with a plan in hand to make this next year great! Both you and your business will enjoy the rewards!

> *Tip: Treat yourself and your business to some quality one-on-one time together. You'll both be the better for it!*

RECOMMENDED READING LIST

[NOTE: Some of these books are out of print, so you may need to check used book websites to find these gems.]

The E-Myth Revisited: Why Most Small Businesses Don't Work and What to Do About It, by Michael E. Gerber

1001 Ways to Motivate Employees, by Bob Nelson

1001 Ways to Reward Employees, by Bob Nelson

Paradigms: The Business of Discovering the Future, by Joel Arthur Barker

Get Clients Now! by C.J. Hayden

Earn What You Deserve, by Jerrold Mundis

How to Work a Room, by Susan Roane

Getting Organized, by Stephanie Winston

Prince Charming Isn't Coming, by Barbara Stanny

Overcoming Underearning, by Barbara Stanny

Secrets of Six-Figure Women, by Barbara Stanny

Why Women Earn Less: How to Make What You're Really Worth, by Mikelann Valterra

Never Eat Alone, by Keith Ferrazzi

Your Road Map to Success, by John C. Maxwell

Who Moved My Cheese, by Spencer Johnson, M.D.

The Tipping Point, by Malcolm Gladwell

Everything by Harry Beckwith

Anything by Ken Blanchard (particularly *Raving Fans*)

INDEX

R

S